KEY TO THE PLAN OF THE SYDNEY UNIVERSITY AND GROUNDS.

1. University Main Building
2. Great Hall
3. Fisher Library
4. Men's Common Room
5. Women's Common Room
6. Medical School
7. Department of Chemistry, Metallurgy, Assaying and Mining
8. Department of Geology and School of Mines
9. Department of Physics
10. Department of Engineering
11. Department of Biology

12. Macleay Museum
13. Gardener's Lodge
14. Messenger's Lodge
15. Caretaker's Lodge
16. Cricket Ground
17. Attendant's Lodge
18. Tennis Courts
19. St. Paul's College
20. St. John's College
21. St. Andrew's College
22. Women's College
23. Prince Alfred Hospital

THE UNIVERSITY OF SYDNEY
1850–1975

THE UNIVERSITY OF SYDNEY

1850 -1975

Some history in pictures
to mark the 125th year of its
incorporation

Chosen and annotated by
G.L.FISCHER, UNIVERSITY ARCHIVIST

SIDERE MENS EADEM MUTATO

THE UNIVERSITY OF SYDNEY, 1975

THE UNIVERSITY OF SYDNEY, 1975

Visitor
His Excellency Sir Roden Cutler, VC, KCMG, KCVO, CBE,
KStJ, Hon.DSc *N.S.W. and N'cle (N.S.W.)*, BEc, Hon.LLD.

Chancellor
Sir Hermann Black, Hon.DLitt *N'cle (N.S.W.)*, MEc, FCIS.

Deputy Chancellor
The Honourable Mr Justice David Mayer Selby, ED, BA, LLB.

Vice-Chancellor and Principal
Professor Bruce Rodda Williams, BA *Melb.*, MA *Adel.*, MA(Econ)
Manc., Hon.DLitt *Keele*.

Deputy Vice-Chancellors
Emeritus Professor William Matthew O'Neil, MA, DipEd.
Professor Michael Gleeson Taylor, MD, BS *Adel.*, PhD Lond., MRACP.

Deputy Principal
Hugh McCredie, LLB, FCIS, FASA.

Registrar
Kenneth Wilson Knight, MEc, PhD *Qld*.

ACKNOWLEDGMENTS

The publication of this book was initiated by The Deputy Principal,
Mr H.McCredie. Most of the illustrations have been drawn from
the pictorial collection in the University Archives which was commenced
by the first University Archivist, Dr D.S.Macmillan, and which
has been built up through the generosity of many donors
within and outside the University. Grateful acknowledgement is also made
to Mr K.Clifford and the staff of the Department of Illustration,
to The Mitchell Library, and to John Fairfax and Sons Ltd.,
for assistance in providing additional illustrations.

ISBN 0 909798 38 9

Designed and printed in Australia by
Edwards & Shaw Pty Ltd, 184 Sussex Street Sydney NSW 2000

Foreword

History, if we accept the suggestion of the late, distinguished, and original, French historian, Marc Bloch, is the answer to questions which each generation asks of the past. Viewed from this perspective, a history of a matter is never finally written, but is always *to be* written; and it is so since new and different questions may come to be asked, and asked even of fields very much ploughed by research.

Hence it is that this collection of pictures of the University of Sydney is not to be taken as "definitive" or "final" in any sense; nor do these pictures foreclose the need to produce further collections, to meet different queries about the past of the University of Sydney, now in its 125th year.

From its necessarily modest inception the University has developed into a large and complex organisation of resources to perform a greatly expanded variety of educational functions; and a glance at a group of current Faculty Handbooks will reveal the diversification of activities of this day and age as against the limited availabilities of academic pursuits in the time of the University's youth. But, in the main, though not wholly, both the expansion, and the innovations which have been part of the University's growth illustrate the many and ever-expanding ways in which two basic functions have been central in the activities of the University of Sydney, namely, teaching in a manner to assist students towards closing the gap between what they know and the bodies of organised knowledge in the many disciplines, and secondly, the widening and deepening of knowledge by research.

But a University, as it grows in age, tends to become venue and source of a great variety of other activities, many of which add colour and introduce memorable occasions into the record of events; or, in current idiom, many and varied are the "happenings" on campus. Some changes and activities are very visible . . . building occurs and and a structure arises, and thus in the earliest years the wits of Sydneytown were quick to remark "Blacket's Folly", as the old buildings fronting the City were dubbed by them. Or, the grounds are shaped and ordered and the whole campus undergoes a "greening".

But other activities are less visible, though none the less significant as part of any answer to a query as to what went on. Hence, the central concept used mainly to guide the selection of and to organise the presentation of this collection of pictures is that of indicating or suggesting University *activities*. This is not to say that the pictures were taken originally with any such concept in the taker's mind. But, like the still and static frames in a strip of film they may well convey the impression of the many activities on the University stage as the viewer turns these pages. Maybe for some it will be a nostalgic journey; for others, an occasion to say merely "so that is how it was"; or yet again, given a minimum of sympathetic, imaginative interpretation, an alumnus, a student, a member of the teaching or the administrative staff could glimpse something of the significant past as they looked before and after; and they might see in embryo what they now do, or sense the real possibility of achieving what they hope to do, encouraged by the record.

Activities mean people, a *dramatis personae,* but this collection does not aim to pass before the viewer's eye all the notable personalities to be found in our archives. A collection of portraits could be the valid objective of a companion volume, as could also be one on the whole furniture of the University, viewed both as buildings and their contents.

Rather the hope inspiring this volume is that these pictures may, in sequence, suggest a range of activities, within the University setting, from sitting for an examination, the angels of the Great Hall impassively aloft, to wreath-carrying, to conferring an honorary degree, to welcoming a Royal visitor, to a myriad of other things, not least the way the Quadrangle encloses in a serene framework of its own, at a silent hour, colour and the play of sunlight, silence and green spaces, with evocative nuances; and how by night it glows and begs the benediction of a contemplative heart, charmed by its simple dignity.

Perforce a selection of scenes, persons, and impedimenta may exclude the one or other well-remembered thing. Perforce, each generation of University folk may recognise familiar things as they look backwards to "their time", and note unfamiliar things, or later developments. The hope is that enough is here rendered in sequence as it is plucked from the record of 125 years, to convey a feeling of the life and growth of the University of Sydney in its manifold activities, within both its historic site and the newer areas of spatial expansion. The University Archivist, Mr Gerald Fischer, brings to this task of selection and assembly of *some* . . . much virtue in "some" . . . of the history of the University of Sydney, the qualities of knowledge and affection, wit and a trace of irony, all admirable equipment for his role; and given the operation of these factors in his assemblage of pictures, done with the aid also of counsel from various folk about the old place, I hope that quiet pleasure may be the harvest of those who view and turn these pages.

Sir Hermann Black
Chancellor

Contents

FRONTISPIECE:

The Great Hall of The University of Sydney, c.1859
Edmund Blacket's crowning glory, inspired by Westminster Hall, London, and rich in carved stone and stained glass. Officially opened on 18 July 1859, The Great Hall perhaps more than any other University building holds the affection of past students and staff. It has a National Trust classification. This watercolor painting (original size 47.5 x 41.5 cm) was done in England by John Blore from details supplied, and shows the original board floor, replaced by marble in 1874. The painting was presented to the University in 1961 by Sir John Nicholson, grandson of Sir Charles Nicholson.

END PAPERS

front: Plan of University Grounds, 1903
back: Plan of University Grounds, 1930

Note on picture captions
Where names of persons are too many to include in caption they have been included in an appendix (p. 132).

PART I

Beginning
1849-1852

In 1849 the population of New South Wales was about 180,000 and of these about a quarter lived in Sydney. Despite the increasing use, greater speed and reliability of steamships linking New South Wales with Great Britain, the lives of all colonists were still greatly affected in many ways by what one historian has termed "the tyranny of distance". For example, those who wished to undertake university education had to suffer a hazardous, costly and lengthy separation from their families in order to attend one of the few universities in Great Britain and no doubt many eligible persons were denied the opportunity because of this. Initial support for the idea of a university in Sydney owed more than a little to the need to overcome this disadvantage. Indeed, for one of the founders, William Charles Wentworth, it was of more than passing concern that colonial youths studying twelve thousand miles away from parental control might become slack and fail to receive "any compensating improvement to their minds".

The idea of establishing a university in Sydney was officially mentioned as early as 1823. In 1831 the Rev. John Dunmore Lang was hopeful that his Australian College might eventually become a university. A more significant development, as it turned out, was the opening of Sydney College, Hyde Park, in 1835, which was also seen as advancing toward something like the status of a university

Sydney Harbour, c.1850 The original of this view is an engraving (7.4 x 10 cm) used by the stationers W. & F.Ford as an advertising bookplate in the University's earliest volume of general correspondence.

8

NEY.

as New South Wales progressed. But though it has been said that the growth of a free population in New South Wales in the 1840's brought about "an increasing sentiment in favour of higher education", secondary education opportunities remained limited and there was apparently no popular clamor for university education.

Just why the years 1849-50 were especially propitious for the establishment of a university, historians have not so far revealed. The return to Australia of Captain Henry Grattan Douglass in October 1848 after twelve years' absence in France certainly appears significant in the timing, for soon after his arrival "the foundation of a University became apparently the chief object of his thought". The people he lobbied advised him to enlist Wentworth's support, which he did. Douglass himself had not been a university undergraduate, though he wrote a medico-scientific thesis which earned him an M.D. from Trinity College, Dublin. It remains a subject of speculation why Grattan made the establishment of a university his own special cause.

Another factor in the timing was that Sydney College had lost support and was at the point of collapse. In 1849 its proprietors, with whom Wentworth was associated, petitioned the New South Wales Government to take over the college and convert it to a university, and it was Wentworth

who moved successfully in the Legislative Council on 6 September 1849 for a Select Committee to enquire into the matter. The report recommended "founding [a university] without any further delay upon a liberal and comprehensive basis . . . which shall be accessible to all classes, and to all collegiate or academical institutions which shall seek its affiliation". A bill to incorporate and endow the University of Sydney was introduced on 2 October 1849 but encountered a number of difficulties, some opponents saying that as it stood it would even allow the appointment of convicts to the Senate. The bill was lost.

There followed a good deal of public comment on the university proposal, church leaders being especially vocal on the matter of provision of religious teaching. The bill was altered and re-introduced in August 1850, and though it successfully retained Clause XX "That no religious test shall be administered to any person in order to entitle him to be admitted as a Student . . . or to hold any office therein", Wentworth had to compromise on the inclusion of four more members of the Senate who would come from four denominations. The second reading of the bill was carried on 11 September and as *An act to incorporate and endow the University of Sydney* it received the Governor's assent on 1 October 1850. In this way the establishment of Australia's first university was authorised.

William Charles Wentworth (1790-1872)
Explorer, statesman, and influential colonist, his support in the N.S.W. Legislative Council was vital to the foundation of the University which he saw as enlightening the minds, refining the understanding and elevating the souls of colonial society; at the same time he believed that the new University should be "open to all, though influenced by none".

Sir Henry Parkes (1815-1896) Premier, statesman and democrat, Parkes alleged through his newspaper *The Empire* that the new university had an "air of aristocratical predilection which with public money ought not to be indulged". Though he had little direct influence on the university, Parkes' introduction of a state school system eventually made it possible for anyone to aspire to University education.

Henry Grattan Douglass (1790-1865)
Douglass, a Dublin-born peripatetic doctor of medicine, and a colonial magistrate, has sometimes been acknowledged as the prime mover in the establishment of the University through his lobbying of Wentworth's support for the project. He was elected to the Senate in 1853 and was a member of the Faculty of Medicine, but in his life-time saw little evidence for his academic optimism.

John Dunmore Lang (1799-1878)
Presbyterian minister, educationist, polemecist and republican, Lang criticised the new University as a "crushing monopoly created in open defiance of the remonstrances, and in supercilious contempt for the opinions of the people". He preferred an American pattern of denominational colleges teaching arts and a University College teaching law, medicine and science, all associated within the University of Sydney. As first envisaged the organisation of the University had some resemblance to Lang's proposal.

NEW SOUTH WALES.

ANNO DECIMO QUARTO

VICTORIÆ REGINÆ.

By His Excellency Sir Charles Augustus Fitz Roy, *Knight Companion of the Royal Hanoverian Guelphic Order, Captain-General and Governor-in-Chief of the Territory of New South Wales and its Dependencies, and Vice-Admiral of the same, with the advice and consent of the Legislative Council.*

No. XXXI.

An Act to Incorporate and Endow the University of Sydney.
[Assented to, 1st October, 1850.]

WHEREAS it is deemed expedient for the better advancement of religion and morality, and the promotion of useful knowledge, to hold forth to all classes and denominations of Her Majesty's subjects resident in the Colony of New South Wales, without any distinction whatsoever, an encouragement for pursuing a regular and liberal course of education : Be it therefore enacted by His Excellency the Governor of New South Wales, with the advice and consent of the Legislative Council thereof, That for the purpose of ascertaining, by means of examination, the persons who shall acquire proficiency in literature, science, and art, and of rewarding them by academical degrees as evidence of their respective attainments, and by marks of honor proportioned thereto, a Senate consisting of the number of persons hereinafter mentioned, shall within three months after the passing of this Act be nominated and appointed by the said Governor, with the advice of the Executive Council of the said Colony, by Proclamation, to be duly published in the *New South Wales Government Gazette*, which Senate shall be and is hereby constituted from the date of such nomination and appointment a Body Politic and Corporate, by the name of " The University of Sydney," by which name such Body Politic shall have perpetual succession, and shall have a common seal, and shall by the same name sue and be sued, implead and be impleaded, and answer and be answered unto in all Courts of the said Colony, and shall be able and capable in law to take, purchase, and hold to them and their successors, all goods, chattels, and personal property whatsoever, and shall also be able and capable in law to take, purchase, and hold to them and their successors, not only such lands, buildings, hereditaments, and possessions

Preamble.

A body politic and corporate, to be named "The University of Sydney," constituted with certain powers.

First page of An Act to Incorporate and Endow The University of Sydney The passage through the N.S.W. Legislative Council of legislation to establish the University was not hurried. A first bill, introduced in October 1849, was lost; after much public comment it was re-introduced in August 1850. It was repealed by The University and University Colleges Act of 1900.

SUPPLEMENT

TO THE

NEW SOUTH WALES

GOVERNMENT GAZETTE,

OF TUESDAY, 24 DECEMBER, 1850.

Published by Authority.

TUESDAY, 24 DECEMBER, 1850.

PROCLAMATION.

By His Excellency SIR CHARLES AUGUSTUS FITZ ROY, Knight Companion of the Royal Hanoverian Guelphic Order, Captain-General and Governor-in-Chief of the Territory of New South Wales and its Dependencies, and Vice-Admiral of the same, &c., &c.

WHEREAS by an Act of the Governor and Legislative Council of New South Wales, passed in the fourteenth year of Her Majesty's Reign, intituled, "*An Act to incorporate and "endow the University of Sydney*," it is amongst other things enacted, that for the purpose of ascertaining by means of examination, the persons who shall acquire proficiency in literature, science, and art, and of rewarding them by Academical Degrees, as evidence of their respective attainments, and by marks of honor proportioned thereto, a Senate, consisting of the number of persons in the said Act mentioned, shall, within three months after the passing thereof, be nominated and appointed by the said Governor, with the advice of the Executive Council of the said Colony, by Proclamation to be duly published in the New South Wales *Government Gazette*, which Senate shall be, and by the said Act is constituted from the date of such nomination and appointment, a Body Politic and Corporate, by the name of "*The University of Sydney*;" and it is thereby further enacted, that the said Body Politic and Corporate shall consist of sixteen Fellows, twelve of whom, at the least, shall be laymen: Now, therefore, I, SIR CHARLES AUGUSTUS FITZ ROY, as such Governor aforesaid, by this my *Proclamation, published in the New

South Wales *Government Gazette*, do notify and proclaim that, with the advice of the said Executive Council, I have nominated and appointed the following persons to be such Senate as aforesaid : that is to say :—

THE REVEREND WILLIAM BINNINGTON BOYCE,
EDWARD BROADHURST, ESQUIRE,
JOHN BAYLEY DARVALL, ESQUIRE,
STUART ALEXANDER DONALDSON, ESQUIRE,
THE RIGHT REVEREND CHARLES HENRY DAVIS,
ALFRED DENISON, ESQUIRE,
EDWARD HAMILTON, ESQUIRE,
JAMES MACARTHUR, ESQUIRE,
FRANCIS LEWIS SHAW MEREWETHER, ESQUIRE,
CHARLES NICHOLSON, ESQUIRE,
BARTHOLOMEW O'BRIEN, ESQUIRE,
THE HONORABLE JOHN HUBERT PLUNKETT, ESQUIRE,
THE REVEREND WILLIAM PURVES,
HIS HONOR ROGER THERRY, ESQUIRE,
THE HONORABLE EDWARD DEAS THOMSON, ESQUIRE,
and
WILLIAM CHARLES WENTWORTH, ESQUIRE.

Given under my Hand and Seal at Government House, Sydney, this twenty-fourth day of December, in the Year of Our Lord one thousand eight hundred and fifty, and in the fourteenth year of Her Majesty's Reign.

(L.S.) CH^{s.} A. FITZ ROY.

By His Excellency's Command,

E. DEAS THOMSON.

GOD SAVE THE QUEEN !

SYDNEY :—Printed by W. W. DAVIES, at the Government Printing Office, 24th December, 1850.

above:

Appointment of first Senate The foundation act provided for a governing Senate of 16 Fellows, at least twelve of whom were to be laymen, thus allowing the appointment of clergymen—a condition to which Wentworth "very grudgingly" consented. To Davis (Roman Catholic), Boyce (Wesleyan), and Purves (Presbyterian) the date of the proclamation may well have seemed auspicious.

The University's first seal The seal (sigillum) represents the University's official corporate signature. It was designed in 1851 by Marshall Claxton and engraved in metal for the hand-stamping of wax impressions. This drawing of the seal shows the symbolic figure of Learning bestowing her laurel wreath on the youth of Australia beneath the Southern Cross and in a bush setting represented by a grass tree. A Latin motto (learning promotes character) was part of the design.

Edward William Terrick Hamilton
(1809-1898) A scholar of Eton and Trinity College Cambridge, wealthy pastoralist and later Agent General for N.S.W. Said to be argumentative and to hold a high opinion of his own abilities, Hamilton was elected as the first Provost (Chancellor) though his attendance at Senate meetings proved infrequent.

Richard Greenup (1803-1866) A Doctor of Medicine of Queen's College Cambridge, Greenup was appointed the first Secretary, Treasurer, Registrar (1850-52) of the University. A man of wide intellectual and public interests, Greenup was fatally stabbed by a patient of the Parramatta lunatic establishment.

Sydney College, College Street, Hyde Park Opened as a private high school in 1835, Sydney College enjoyed success for some years but its closure c.1848 prompted its proprietors to petition the Government to convert it to a University. Though the offer was not taken up the property was later acquired by the University.

13

The College St. premises in 1974
Occupied by Sydney Grammar School since 1857, the central part of the 1835 building ("Big School") survives. The wings on either side are later additions designed by E.T.Blacket.

below:

Inauguration of The University of Sydney, Monday 11 October 1852, at 11 p.m. Held in the hall of the College St. premises, the inauguration was combined with the first matriculation ceremony at which 24 students were enrolled. In the presence of the Governor-General, Sir Charles FitzRoy, the Vice-Provost (Sir Charles Nicholson) announced the commencement of the "first academic courses" and the Principal (Professor John Woolley) spoke of the idea of the University as a "school of liberal and general knowledge". This illustration was published in *The Illustrated London News* of 29 January 1853.

	Filius.	Ortu.	Educatus.	Annos Natus.	Habitat.
Wentworth, Fitzwilliam	Gulielmi Caroli	Sidneiensis	apud Vir: rev: H. Carey	XIX	apud Patrem
Leary, Georgius	Joannis	ed.	in Collegio Sidneiensi	XXII	apud se
Leary, Josephus	Joannis	id	id	XXI	apud se
Johnson, Jacobus Gulielmus	Roberti	id	apud Vir. rev. H. Casey	XVIII	apud Patrem
Allen, Eurelus	Georgi	id	apud Vir Doct. Woolls	XV	apud Patrem
Riley, Alexander Raby	Gulielmi Edv	id	apud eundem	XIX	apud Tutorem
Windeyer, Gulielmus Carolus	Ricardi	Londinensis	in Schola Regia Tanamaticali	XVIII	apud se
Wilson, Jacobus Offiiatt	Caroli	Sidneiensis	in Collegio Sidneiensi	XVI	apud Patrem
Hirst, Gulielmus Henricus Abbott	Gulielmi	id	apud Vir. Rev. H. Carey	XV	apud Tutorem
Forshall, Gulielmus Hui	Josiæ	Londinensis	in Collegio B. Petri Westminsteriensi	XXII	apud Tutorem
Moore, Gulielmus Andreas	Josephi	Sidneiensis	in Collegio Sidneiensi	XVIII	apud Patrem
Kinloch, Joannes	Joannis	Dubliniensis	apud vir. rev. Fullerton	XX	apud Patrem
Curtis, Gulielmus Cyprian	Jacobi	Sidneiensis	in seminario B. Mariæ Virg. apud Sidneiam	XIX	apud Patrem
Sealy, Robertus	Joannis	Corcensis	in Coll: rev: trin: juxta Dub.	XXI	apud Tutorem
Fitzgerald, Robertus Marsden	Roberti	Sidneiensis	in Collegio Sidneiensi	XVI	apud Tutorem
Oliver, Alexander	Andreæ	id	apud vir Doct: J. J. Cape	XIX	apud Tutorem
Kindur, Rodney	Vir. Wm. Campbell	id	apud eundem	XVI	apud Patrem
Burdekin, Marshall	Thomæ	id	apud eundem	XV	apud Matrem
Willis, Robertus e par	Josephi	Anglus, ex agro Suthriensi	apud eundem	XV	apud Patrem
Lee, Edvardus	Gulielmi	Bathurstianus	apud eundem	XV	apud Tutorem
Mitchell, David Scott	Jacobi	Sidneiensis	apud Vir Rev. N. Grylls	XVI	apud Patrem
Radford, Henricus Wyatt	Henrici	id	apud Vir Doct. Woolls	XVII	apud Tutorem
Clarke, Thomas B	Thomæ	natus in insula quæ vocatur Beata Lucia apud Ind: occidentales	apud eundem	XX	apud Patrem
Coulson, Thomas Henricus	Thomæ	Sidneiensis	in Collegio Sidneiensi	XVIII	apud Matrem

Roll of the first matriculants A necessary part of the 1852 matriculation ceremony was the enrolment of the students in an official register. The use of Latin preserved a link with medieval tradition and gave added solemnity to the record. The large page size (51 x 37 cm) is typical of some early university records.

Register of Fees

1852		Received as Lecture fees. from Matriculated Students from					
Oct	14ᵗʰ	David Scott Mitchell	£	6	6	.	
"	"	Frederick Hale Forshall	£	4	4	.	
"	"	Charles Allen		6	6	.	
"	"	Fitzwilliam Wentworth		6	6	.	
"	"	George Leary		6	6	.	
"	"	Joseph Leary		6	6	..	
"	"	W H Abbott Hirst		4	4	.	
"	"	John Kinloch		6	6	.	
"	"	W. Cyprian Curtis		6	6	.	
"	"	Jacob Affriatt Wilson		6	6	.	58	16	.
"	15	Robert Speir Willis		4	4	.	
"	"	Edward Lee		6	6	.	
"	"	Rodney Riddell		6	6	.	
"	"	Alexander Raby Riley		6	6	.	
"	"	Marshall Burdikin		6	6	.	
"	"	William Charles Windeyer		6	6	.	
"	"	Henry Wyatt Radford		6	6	.	42	0
"	18	Alexander Oliver		4	4	.	
"	18	James W. Johnson		4	4	.	
"	18	Robert Marsden Fitzgerald		4	4	.	
"	28	Thomas H Coulton		6	6	.	
"	28	W. Andrew Moore		4	4	..	
"	28	Robert Sealy		4	4		27	6

Register of first lecture fees—14 October 1852
Undergraduates paid £2.2.0 ($4.20) each term for each course of lectures—classics, mathematics, physics; part of this fee was paid to the professors and lecturers. Lectures were given daily between 9 a.m. and 1 p.m., Mondays to Saturdays, and the by-laws required them to be at least one hour in length.

John Woolley, M.A., D.C.L., Oxon.
(1816-1866) A student of the Universities of
London and Oxford, a Church of England
priest, and a schoolmaster, Woolley arrived
in Sydney on 9 July 1852 to become the first
Principal and Professor of Classics. He was
to be disappointed at the slow growth of the
University and at Anglican criticism of his
part as Principal. He was drowned at sea while
returning to Australia from England.

Morris Birkbeck Pell, B.A., Cantab.
(1827-1879) At the age of 25 Pell arrived
in Sydney on 9 July 1852 to become the first
Professor of Mathematics. A Senior Wrangler
and Fellow of St. John's College Cambridge,
his teaching work with students is said to have
offered little challenge to his abilities because
of the lack of secondary education.

right:

John Smith, C.M.G., M.A., M.D., Aberdeen
(1821-1885) The son of a blacksmith, Smith
arrived in Sydney on 8 September 1852 to
become the first Professor of Chemistry and
Experimental Physics. Described as a leader of
scientific progress in Australia he was an
advocate in 1866 of an association of
Australian scientists. His photographs of the
University under construction in the 1850's
are an important pictorial record.

17

PART II

Surviving
1853-1881

The new university was a modest enterprise. It had only three professors, twenty-four matriculated students, one faculty—Arts, and an annual grant of £5,000 ($10,000), and over the next thirty years there was little change in all these factors. By 1881 only one more professor had been appointed (for mineralogy), there were two lecturers (Latin and mathematics), a demonstrator in chemistry (who swore in German when the primitive water supply failed in his laboratory), the number of first year students was thirty-seven, and the Government grant had only just been increased to £6,000 ($12,000). The Government, of course, had been generous in other ways: it had provided the Grose

Water pump under Great Tower During the period 1852 to 1881 the University was as parched for funds as it was for water. This pump provided the one reliable water supply drawn from a nearby underground tank which was in turn fed from the Main Building roof; attendant staff "had the pleasure of carrying the water in buckets for the students needs".

Farm site and met the cost of the great pile of Victorian Gothic Revival buildings that arose there. But it had been a somewhat patrician and university-minded Legislative Council that had initiated this expenditure; perhaps the needs of the University did not appear so pressing to the democratically elected governments after 1856. Some private benefactions were beginning to come in but they were relatively modest amounts, often earmarked for scholarships and prizes. The public had also generously subscribed to the erection of buildings for three denominational colleges during this period.

The Senate had originally proposed that the University of Sydney should be an examining body and that all instruction would be given by the three professors in its own University College of which Woolley would be Principal. Despite their short acquaintance of each other and their different backgrounds, upon taking up their chairs, Woolley, Smith and Pell displayed an impressive degree of academic solidarity in opposing this plan. It was their view that they should be Professors of the University and that all matriculated students should attend their lectures, and the Senate accepted this change.

The curriculum for undergraduates was rigorous and narrow—classics (Greek and Latin), mathematics, chemistry and experimental philosophy (physics); in their third year students specialised in one or two of these subjects for honours passes. There were some experiments with lectures in logic, jurisprudence, French and German, but the last two had to be abandoned because of the poor entrance standard of students wishing to take them. In the field of mathematics it has been said that Pell was rarely extended by the general ability of his students. In 1866, prompted by a practical recognition of the country's potential mineral and energy resources, a Reader (later Professor) in Geology was appointed. From 1855 the University was authorised to examine in law and medicine and degrees were granted in these latent faculties from the mid-1860's. The conferring of as many as thirteen doctorates in law by 1881 suggests that the academic *cachet* of a higher degree was well recognised at this time.

In such a small community even those students who did not live in colleges were able to enjoy something like a college atmosphere in their close relations with their teachers. For those who were in the colleges there was the advantage of tutorial assistance, but life could be spartan, disciplined, and the plumbing primitive. In the interests of students who had to live in boarding houses or

lodgings the Act of Incorporation required the Provost (Chancellor) and Vice-Provost to keep a watchful eye for undesirable surroundings, indifferent tutors and rapacious masters. Within a decade of the inauguration, undergraduates were already leaving their own impress on the history of the University. Football and cricket clubs were formed in the early 1860's, though sometimes including graduates in their teams and management. In 1874 the Sydney University Union was formed to promote the "mental culture" of its members through debates and a magazine, and a musical society had been formed by 1878.

Though large popular crowds often attended the Saturday morning Commemoration and Conferring of Degrees ceremonies, the University in this period tended to be isolated from the general community, the severe and elevated grandeur of its building and its unkempt grounds seeming to emphasise this isolation. Both Woolley, and Badham who succeeded him as Principal, tried to dispel this isolation through public lectures and offers of study help by correspondence. All the professors were involved in public education and local learned societies, and John Smith went so far as to become a member of the Legislative Council for a time. Badham's successful move to banish Latin from the University's ceremonies was possibly motivated by his desire to make the University less esoteric in the mind of the public. But all these efforts were apparently only of limited effectiveness in combating the opinion that the University had "failed to produce the benefits anticipated from it". The University did confer one important benefit when it set up a system of public examinations in 1867, thus establishing itself as the arbiter of standards of public education and at the same time helping to formulate and improve those standards.

However, it was Henry Parkes' Public Instruction Act of 1880, bringing secondary education to boys and girls in a much wider area of the community, that was responsible for injecting new life and change into the University. Not only were more students enabled to present themselves for matriculation, but there followed a growing demand for graduates as teachers for the new education system. Two other significant events combined with this development to mark the year 1881 as a watershed in University history. In 1880 John Henry Challis, a wealthy Sydney merchant, died leaving his vast estate to the University, and in 1881 the Senate approved the admission of women to the University. Fed with increasing numbers of students and nourished with Challis funds, the University could now turn from the struggle to survive to the problems of growing.

University premises in College St., Hyde Park
The University acquired Sydney College in
1851 and held its classes here until 1857; in
its hall the first Bachelor of Arts degrees were
conferred in 1856. In 1855 the building was
sold to the Trustees of Sydney Grammar
School for £12,000, though the University
continued to occupy it until its new premises
became available.

w *CATHOLIC CHAPEL.*   DARL.

20

HURST.
Park.

SYDNEY COLLEGE AS COMPLETED

The University Mace Presented to the University in the name of Queen Victoria by the Governor-General, Sir Charles FitzRoy, the mace was apparently paid for by the University. Made of silver by Sydney craftsmen of Brush and McDonnell, it was received by the University at the end of 1854 though lacking the University's arms which had not been granted at that time. The symbol of the Senate's authority, the mace is carried on ceremonial occasions by the Esquire Bedell.

Hugh Kennedy (1829-1882) Appointed Registrar and Secretary in 1853 (after the brief office of W.L.Hutton), Kennedy held the position until his death. A scholar of Balliol College, Oxford, he also lectured in classics to students who thought him "more ornamental than useful".

An Annual Certificate of 1853 The Principal of the University, Professor John Woolley, testifies (in Latin) that William Charles Windeyer, an undergraduate, has satisfactorily completed through attendance and examinations, a full year in Arts as required by the University statutes.

UNIV. SIDN.

Term. Trin. A.S. MDCCC*LIII*

Windeyer Gul. Car. quam integrum annum in studio Artium posuerit, Professores Publicos diligenter audiverit, Examinatorum Academicorum quæstionibus satis responderit, cætera, prout statuta requirunt, peregerit; annum studiorum suorum tram , sive terminos *III* , rite complevisse testamur.

Ioan. Woolley J. C. P.

Principalis.

Hugo. Kennedy.
Registrarius.

View from the Grose Farm Site, 1850's The
present main site of the University was
originally part of a Crown Reserve, some of
which was from 1792 granted to the
Lieut.-Governor, Major Francis Grose, hence
the name Grose Farm. Later the site formed
part of a grant to the Orphan Institution.
Recognising the restriction of the College St.
site, the Senate in 1853 negotiated with the
Government for the Grose Farm site and in
1855 received 128 acres under deed of grant,
some of which was later sub-granted to the
colleges.

David Scott Mitchell (1836-1907)
A foundation matriculant, B.A. 1856 and
M.A. 1859, Mitchell was once admonished by
the Senate for neglecting his studies and
offering a blank examination paper in physics.
But his behaviour was partly excused on the
ground that as a colonial he lacked that
English public school background which
encouraged "habits of thought, industry,
perseverance and general intellectual activity".
Mitchell's collection of books and manuscripts
later belied this view and they now form the
basis of The Mitchell Library.

*William Charles Windeyer (1834-1897) as an
undergraduate* One of the first matriculants
and the senior of the first Bachelor of Arts
graduates in 1856, Windeyer found himself at
examination times "tremendously busy with all
imaginable philosophies to read". His
association with the University was long and
close—M.A. 1859, Member of Parliament for
the University 1876-79, Fellow of the Senate,
and as Judge Sir William Windeyer he was
Chancellor 1895-96.

The Wentworth Medal—1854 In 1854
W.C.Wentworth gave £200 to found an
annual prize for the best English essay. The
prize in the form of a medal was awarded to
W.C.Windeyer in 1854 and again in 1855.
The photographs show the 1854 medal bearing
the head of the Greek goddess Athena,
and the inscription on the reverse.

UNIVERSITY

28

OF SYDNEY.

The University of Sydney: an impression by Richard Ransome, c.1856 In 1853 a building sub-committee of the Senate reported on the accommodation to be built at the Grose Farm site and recommended an "Elizabethan style" because it allowed "indefinite extension without impairing its general effect as a whole". Early in 1854 E.T.Blacket was engaged as the University's architect. This very early engraving (original size 22.5 x 34.2 cm) is possibly based on Blacket's original plans which have not survived.

Part of the first Graduate Register—1856 Out of 24 original matriculants, only 7 graduated in the normal course of 3 years. They were required to subscribe to a Latin promise that they would observe the statutes and promote the peace of the University, a practice continued until 1970.

Edmund Thomas Blacket (1817-1883) Blacket resigned as N.S.W. Colonial Architect in 1854 to design and supervise the Main Building and Great Hall of the University. The grand scale of these buildings constitutes his major work and is perhaps the most notable piece of Gothic Revival architecture in Australia. Blacket is shown with his sister, c.1858, the Great Hall in course of building.

The Great Tower in course of building, c.1857
Completed in the early 1860's, the Great
Tower displayed a single face clock, the gift
of Sir Stuart Donaldson, an original Fellow
of the Senate. This photograph was probably
made by Professor John Smith.

right:

Blacket's proposal for Great Tower, c.1855
Blacket's plans and drawings for the University
have not survived except for a few minor
items. This is one of several rejected designs
for the completion of the Great Tower.

The Main Building, c.1857 Parts of the Main Building were used for classes from October 1857, and as Principal, Woolley lived on the premises from 1858 until his death. This rare early photograph shows the three foundation professors picking their way through the rising grandeur. (L. to R.) Smith, Pell, Woolley.

right:

The University from Parramatta Road, c.1860 A distant view of the Main Building and Great Hall from a point near present-day Grace Bros. In 1860 expenditure on the final details of the Great Tower was deferred in favour of a small museum for antiquities; at the same time, a Parliamentary Select Committee wondered if the "monstrous shapes" of gargoyles which decorated the building would ever assist the development of "a high type of architectural taste".

Victoria by the Grace of God

By Warrant under the Queen's Sign Manual

C. Romilly

Royal Charter of 27 February 1858 Through this document, issued by the authority of the home Government, degrees awarded by The University of Sydney were recognised as having the same standing as degrees awarded by universities in Great Britain. The document is of a type called Letters Patent, and the original engrossed parchment measures 22.7 x 30 cm. Queen Victoria's Great Seal (made of wax, approx. 14.75 cm dia.) was originally fixed to the document by cords but was later housed separately for safekeeping.

Grant of Arms to the University of Sydney from the College of Heralds, London, 14 May 1857 Adopted by the Senate on 13 December 1856 the arms incorporate the open book of Oxford and the Royal lion of Cambridge with the local symbolism of the Southern Cross of stars. The shield is silver, the cross azure, the stars gold, the lion gold on a red background. The Latin motto *Sidere mens eadem mutato* is attributed to Francis Merewether, an original Fellow of the Senate, though it may have been suggested by the Epistles of Horace. Its meaning "Though the stars are changed our spirit is the same" implies that the tradition of ancient universities will be continued in Australia.

SIDERE MENS EADEM MUTATO

TO ALL AND SINGULAR

to whom these Presents shall come Sir Charles George Young Knight GARTER Principal King of Arms James Pulman Esquire CLARENCEUX King of Arms and Robert Laurie Esquire NORROY King of Arms Send Greeting Whereas Sir Charles Nicholson Knight Provost of the University of SYDNEY hath by Letter represented unto the Most Noble Henry Granville Duke of Norfolk Earl Marshal and Hereditary Marshal of England That in an Act passed by the Parliament of New South Wales in the month of October 1850 and subsequently approved by Her Most Gracious Majesty Queen Victoria it was enacted by His Excellency the Governor of New South Wales with the advice and consent of the Legislative Council thereof that for the better advancement of religion and morality and the promotion of useful knowledge and to hold forth to all classes and denominations of Her Majesty's Subjects resident in the Colony of New South Wales without any distinction whatsoever an encouragement for pursuing a regular and liberal course of education and for other purposes therein declared a Body Politic and Corporate be created by the Name of The University of SYDNEY and by which Name such Body Politic should have perpetual Succession and should have a Common Seal and should by the same Name sue and be sued implead and be impleaded and answer and be answered unto in all Courts of the said Colony. That the Senate of the said University being desirous that Armorial Ensigns should be assigned under His Grace's Authority He therefore requested on behalf of the said Senate that His Grace would issue His Warrant for the granting and assigning such Arms as may be proper to be borne by the said University of Sydney on Seals Shields or otherwise according to the Laws of Arms And forasmuch as the said Earl Marshal did by Warrant under His hand and seal bearing date the twelfth day of May instant authorize and direct Us to grant and assign such Arms accordingly Know Ye therefore that We the said GARTER CLARENCEUX and NORROY in pursuance of His Grace's Warrant and by virtue of the Letters Patent of Our several Offices to each of Us respectively granted do by these Presents grant and assign unto the said University of SYDNEY the Arms following that is to say Argent on a Cross Azure an open book proper, clasps Gold, between four Stars of eight points Or, on a chief Gules a Lion passant guardant also Or, together with this motto "Sidere mens eadem mutato" as the same are in the Margin hereof more plainly depicted to be borne and used for ever hereafter by the said University of SYDNEY on their Common Seal Shields or otherwise according to the Laws of Arms. In Witness whereof we the said GARTER CLARENCEUX and NORROY Kings of Arms have to these Presents subscribed Our names and affixed the Seals of Our several Offices this fourteenth day of May in the Twentieth year of the Reign of Our sovereign Lady Victoria by the Grace of God of the United Kingdom of Great Britain and Ireland Queen Defender of the Faith &c and in the year of Our Lord One thousand eight hundred and fifty seven.

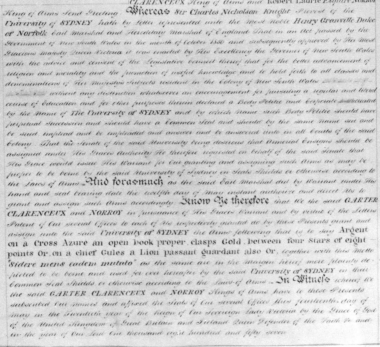

F. C. TERRY

View from Parramatta Road, c.1860's In this water-colour by F.C.Terry the University is distantly seen from the west with St. John's College on the right.

Undergraduates c.1857 The earliest photograph of its kind in the University Archives, and possibly taken at the College St. premises. The group includes H.C.Russell B.A. 1859) who later became N.S.W. Government Astronomer; he is possibly the central figure.

Undergraduates c.1859 Photographed near the entrance to the northern vestibule of the Main Building. Students of this time were required to wear "plain black stuff" gowns and trencher caps, a velvet band on the sleeve distinguishing the scholars. Fellows, professors and senior officers had to be saluted respectfully.

The University grounds, c.1870 This view looks north-east to the Main Building and Great Hall still surrounded by pastures.

Unknown boy, possibly c.1880 From his apron, this boy could be an apprentice or young attendant. He stands before the north vestibule doorway whose stone step is already well worn by two generations of students.

Northern door of Main Building, c.1859 Both north and south doors were originally decorated with Latin mottos. Above this door is "Voluntas arcus facta saggittae" ("The will is the bow, the deeds are the arrows".) It is said that Professor Charles Badham, exasperated by requests to give its meaning, ordered its removal.

Sir Charles Nicholson Bt. (1808-1903) A founder and benefactor, Vice-Provost and Chancellor 1851-62, Sir Charles Nicholson's interest in the University was warmly held throughout his life. The Royal Charter and Grant of Arms were obtained largely through his efforts, and his many gifts formed the nucleus of the Nicholson Museum of Antiquities. This photograph is of the Phillips portrait in the Great Hall.

The Great Hall and The Angel of Knowledge, 1870 The spirit of the University was symbolised by Blacket in a carved stone Angel of Knowledge set on a pedestal above the entrance gable. Its removal as soon as 1874 points up the academic moral of knowledge unsoundly based.

Saint Paul's College and The University, 1870
It was accepted at the time of foundation that denominational colleges would be associated with the University and in 1854 an act authorised their establishment and endowment. The first building was St. Paul's Anglican College, commenced in 1856.

Entrance Drive from Newtown Road, c.1870
An impressive, if largely unmade, drive led from Newtown (City) Road to the Great Tower gate entrance; ornate gates, a wooden bridge and noble trees lent later dignity up to 1924 when the University's boundaries were altered. A Sydney Council proposal at the same time to extend Cleveland St. through the Park to Parramatta Road was strongly opposed by the University generally.

left:

Edmund Barton (1849-1920) As an undergraduate Barton studied classics, mathematics, physics, French and law. He was a Scholar and Prizeman and graduated B.A. in 1868 and M.A. in 1870. A keen supporter of the Cricket Club and a Fellow of the Senate for many years, Barton became Australia's first Prime Minister.

The University from Parramatta Road, c.1870
The Great Tower has been completed and a gate-house erected at the road entrance.

St PAUL'S COLLEGE & UNIVERSITY
SYDNEY NOV 1870

A University football team, 1871 An official University history implies that a Rugby Union team was formed in 1863 but the claim has been disputed. This photograph was taken outside the Main Building. (For list of names, see Appendix.)

Oxford Hotel, King St., Sydney This was the scene of the Sydney University Union's inaugural meeting in 1874 under the chairmanship of R.E.O'Connor. Regular debates on parliamentary lines were later held in the old Public Library on the west side of Macquarie Street.

The Chancellor's Memorandum on the admission of women, 6 April 1881 Regarded from its inception as a male preserve, the University did not specifically exclude women, though it required the support of the Chancellor, Sir William Manning, to achieve their admission in fact. This event marked a significant change from the old order though male exclusiveness died hard.

Memorandum - read by the Chancellor in support of his motion, in the admission of women to University, privileges

April 8th 1881.

It appears to me very desirable that steps should be taken by the Senate - without further delay - for the extension to women of the advantages of high education under the auspices of the University.

The following occur to me as the more prominent reasons for this course

1. In a political sense, both sexes have an equal right to participate in these advantages, seeing that this University has been founded for the general benefit of the Public, and is maintained at the general public cost.

2. I apprehend that there is nothing in the Statutes of this University which is opposed to this equality in favour of women

3. Socially, I see no reason why such women as may be ambitious of and competent to attain the higher education of the University, and desirous of receiving its distinctions, should not be admitted to full participation in the advantages it offers; save only that there may be a necessity for some differences of study, both on account of the greater delicacy of the sex and of considerations of greater appropriateness to the course of life open to women

4. The tendency of modern opinions on this question, and the example set by other Universities both at home and in some British Colonies, appear to render it almost imperative that we should open our own University to women equally with Men.

(Signed) W. M. Manning
Chancellor

Academic staff and third year students, 1881
The old order on the edge of change: of the three original professors only John Smith remains, though the academic staff is little enlarged and the number of first year students (37) not much increased from 1852. (L. to R. front row) Professor Theodore Gurney (mathematics), Professor ʾArchibald Liversidge (chemistry and mineralogy), Canon Robert Allwood (Vice-Chancellor), Professor Charles Badham (classics), and Professor John Smith (experimental physics).

PART III

Growing
1882 - 1945

When Sir Mungo MacCallum died in 1942 the Senate's minute of appreciation of his life and service recorded that "he arrived [in 1887] as a harbinger of that new age in which the University, more amply endowed, earned and attained a worth and status comparable with those of all but the oldest of British Universities". MacCallum had come to Sydney partly out of a desire to play a part in the development of a country which had excited his admiration by its demonstration of loyalty in the Sudan war a few years earlier, and his long and influential association with the University was almost coterminous with the period of this section. The years 1882-1945 were indeed more amply endowed (though never sufficiently so to meet all the demands made on the University) and characterised by wide-ranging growth and a strong sense of traditional loyalty.

Challis' bequest finally amounted to about £250,000 ($500,000) and made possible chairs and lectureships in modern literature, law, history, engineering, biology, anatomy, logic and mental philosophy. In 1885, Thomas Fisher's bequest of £30,000 ($60,000) greatly assisted the development of the Library, and in 1896 Sir Peter Nicol Russell gave the first of two £50,000 ($100,000) endowments to the Engineering School. Increased support from the Government of New South Wales was more conservatively in bricks and mortar to back up the new academic appointments. With the exception of the first Fisher Library which was sited to balance Blacket's Great Hall and contribute to the completion of the Quadrangle, the new buildings like the Medical School and the Macleay Museum do not seem to have conformed to any over-all plan for the grounds. In 1915 Walter Burley Griffin had been asked to submit a plan for the future development of the grounds, but it was not adopted, nor was that of the University's own Professor of Architecture, Leslie Wilkinson, in 1920.

With increased funds, staff and facilities, the University was at last able to reach out to a larger section of the public. Evening lectures in Arts began in 1884, the University Extension Board was set up in 1892 to bring University teaching "within the reach of men and women who are unable to attend the University", and in 1914 a

Department of Tutorial Classes was established in association with the Workers' Educational Association to provide adult education services. The University's own range of formal instruction was broadened and new degree and diploma courses were made available. Some of these—engineering (1882), mining and metallurgy (1892), and departments of agriculture and veterinary science (1909)—were clearly related to the basic economy of New South Wales; others, like architecture (1917), and oriental studies (1919) had cultural as well as practical applications. Experiments were made with technical-type diploma courses—military studies (1906), economics and commerce (1907), and journalism in the early 1920's — though some of these were soon abandoned.

This increased activity and a growth of student numbers (90 in 1881, 583 in 1900, over 3,300 in 1920) called for new academic and administrative structures. The Faculty of Science had been established in 1882 but had become something of a catch-all for those departments like engineering, architecture and agriculture which did not seem to fit in the other faculties—Arts, Law and Medicine. In 1919, Sir Samuel McCaughey's bequest of almost £500,000 ($1m) made possible many new appointments and was thus a kind of catalyst in the formation of six new faculties — engineering, economics, architecture, dentistry, agriculture and veterinary science. The faculties, together with the Professorial Board (established in 1886) were responsible for the academic administration of the University, but judging from the minutes of these bodies they met briefly and infrequently. In such a small university community there was perhaps little need to meet often; in any case, the Senate continued to exercise a dominant authority in all University matters. It was not until 1941 that the custom was firmly established of making academic appointments only on the recommendation of the Professorial Board. Breaches of student discipline were dealt with by the Proctorial Board, though most serious incidents up to 1945 seemed to come up in relation to "Commem." Day behaviour in the city. The growing administrative complexity of the University was recognised in 1924 by the appointment of a full-time Vice-Chancellor as the Chief Executive Officer of the University; he was assisted by the Registrar and a staff of 18 officers.

In the Great War of 1914-18, MacCallum saw at first hand a new flowering of that patriotism which he had so admired in the 1880's. There was a heavy enlistment of staff, students and graduates, but the war did not directly interrupt general university life, and some major building projects (for Agriculture, the Library, and the cloisters) were completed during the period. Even so, the memory of the war and the realisation of the vast loss of life it incurred, were deeply felt in university life in the 1920's and 1930's. The War Memorial Carillon appeal enjoyed wide popular support, and Anzac Day and Armistice Day were occasions of solemn ceremonies; some members of staff stood stiffly to attention on all occasions when the carillon played *God Save the King* and were outraged at the sight of those who did not.

A more direct threat to the University was posed by the economic depression of the early 1930's. The Government of N.S.W. reduced its grant from £74,000 ($148,000) to just under £52,900 ($105,800), and the Senate reduced salaries and wages by a flat rate of ten per cent. The Vice-Chancellor conveyed the Senate's "cordial thanks to members of the staff for their co-operation and assistance in the existing financial stringency". Evening lectures in science were suspended as a further economy measure. In the worst years of the depression the enrolment was a little over 3,000 but from the mid-1930's numbers began to increase and reached about 3,700 in 1939. As world political events moved toward the second world war students in 1938 might have discerned with mild irony the latest course changes that on the one hand set up a chair of aeronautical engineering, the newest technology of destruction, and on the other introduced a degree course in divinity, one of the oldest university studies.

48

Grave of John Henry Challis (1806-1880)
Challis' Australian merchant fortune was made by 1855 when he left to live in Europe. He married only a few years before his death at Mentone, France, and was buried at Folkestone, Kent. The estate of about £250,000 did not come in to the University until 1889.

Conferring degrees in the 1880's From 1859 conferring of degrees ceremonies were usually held in the Great Hall on Saturdays at mid-day. Until 1869 they were conducted in Latin in the tradition of ancient English universities, the Fellows of the Senate '"delivering their placet" (approval) in person. This illustration shows Sir William Manning, Chancellor 1878-95.

Miss Jane Foss Russell, c.1887 The daughter of H.C.Russell (B.A. 1859), Miss Russell graduated as Bachelor of Arts in 1886 with 1st class honours in classics. In 1892 she was appointed Tutor to women students and she later married H.E.Barff, the Registrar.

University Football Team, 1882 Back row: Roberts, Addison, Shaw, Raper; 3rd row: Metcalfe, Tange, Baker; 2nd row: Barry, Rygate, C., Mann, Bayliss; kneeling: Elphinstone, McManamey; front row: Amess, Bennett, Rygate, P., Flynn, Beegling. This team includes graduates, undergraduates, and perhaps some players from outside the University.

Student's Room, St. Andrew's College, 1880's Moves to found a Presbyterian College were made in the 1850's but the College Council was not formed until 1870. The College opened in 1876 and in the mid-1880's had 22 undergraduate students.

REGISTRARS ROOM, SYDNEY UNIVERSITY.

The Registrar's Office, c.1905 After Professor Badham's death in 1884 the rooms he had as living quarters in the Main Building were put to other uses; one (now the Greek lecture room) became the Registrar's Office, the general administrative centre of the University. In the 1890's the Registrar's staff comprised the Chief Clerk (Accountant) and one clerk.

left:

Henry Ebenezer Barff (1857-1925) Born in Tahiti, Barff graduated B.A. in 1876 and was appointed Master of Studies. In 1882 he graduated M.A. and was appointed Registrar, and in 1914 he was also made Warden. Said to have "perhaps just a little more power than was appropriate to his office", Barff's role bore some resemblance to that of an executive Vice-Chancellor, and to this he added the post of Librarian.

Sir Anderson Stuart (1856-1920) Thomas Peter Anderson Stuart came from Scotland in 1883 to establish the medical school as Professor of Anatomy and Physiology; his achievements in securing a new building (now bearing his name), promoting the teaching of dentistry, and his interest in the university grounds were equally significant.

2nd Year Medical Students, 1886
Photographed outside the Main Building, this group is notable for the presence of Miss Dagmar Berne (d.1900), the first woman medical student. Others in the group are: J.M.McInnes, F.C.S.Shaw, H.R.Nolan, J.T.Wilson (Demonstrator in Anatomy), J.Morton, H.Lister, C.G.Wilson, G.Morton, W.J.Shirlow, L.E.F.Neill, F.Badham, P.L.Townley, Miss Berne, E.H.Binney, and C.Purser.

right:

The first medical school building Until 1889 the work of the medical school was housed in this small cottage near the site of the present Old Union, Science Road. Small as it was, Anderson Stuart had to share it with other lecturers whom he drove out with medical odours. The original of this wood print is 3.2 cm across.

*Aeschylus' Agamemnon in the Great Hall,
1886* With the help of the Professor of
Classics, Walter Scott, an all-male student cast
played a two-night season of this tragedy—
in Greek. R.R.Garran (centre) was
Agamemnon, on his right is Cassandra
(G.H.Leibius), and on his left, Clytemnestra
(H.A.Russell). The venture showed a loss of
£30 ($60).

Anderson Stuart's Private Room, c.1900
Through Anderson Stuart's drive, teaching of
medicine was transferred in 1890 to the
building which now bears his name. His own
private room there exhibits the warmth of
coal fire and carpet, and the influence of
primitive, classical, and religious art.

*Professor Anderson Stuart transmogrified,
c.1912* A "Commem." Day student with false
nose achieves a rare degree of sartorial
verisimilitude, not overlooking the delicately
held cigarette.

Mungo William MacCallum (1854-1942)
In 1886 MacCallum was appointed Professor
of Modern Literature, and in 1924 he became
the first executive Vice-Chancellor. He was
knighted in 1926, elected Deputy-Chancellor
in 1928, and was Chancellor 1934-36. A
student recalls that MacCallum wrote a
dreadful diagonal hand, spoke of a play called
The Marrrchant of Venice, and combined
scholarship and administration in an
outstanding way. This sketch is from the
undergraduate magazine *Hermes* of 1890.

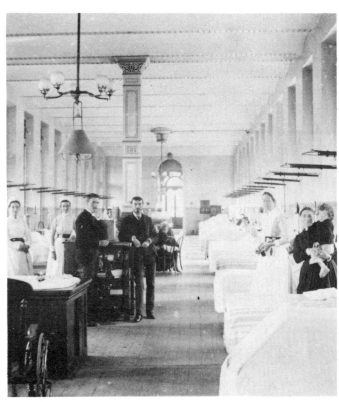

right:

*Children's Ward in Royal Prince Alfred
Hospital, probably before 1900* The hospital
opened in 1882, built on land resumed from
the University grant. The medical staff was
appointed by a conjoint board of the Hospital
and the University and students from the
University received clinical training in the
hospital. In 1886 the hospital agreed to
establish a children's ward for the teaching of
clinical diseases.

St Johns College N.S.W

The Library, 1887 From 1857 to 1908 the Library was housed on the first floor of the Main Building in what is now the Senate Room. The first Librarian was F.H.Forshall; at this time Ralph Hardy was the Assistant Libarian. Furniture and shelves seen in this photograph are still in active use.

Physics (left) and Chemistry (right) buildings, 1893 Much altered the Physics Building (later Electrical Engineering) is now the Badham Building; the Chemistry Building is incorporated in the Pharmacy complex. This photograph is one of many by Archibald Liversidge (1846-1927), appointed Professor of Geology and Mineralogy in 1874, and later Professor of Chemistry.

St. John's Catholic College, 1880's The second of the church colleges, St. John's opened in 1862. William Wardell's Gothic design included an elaborate tower which was not built; a modified design of the tower was completed during 1937-39.

58

Chemistry Class, 1896 For many years an unwritten law required women students to sit in front rows; yet some academics persisted in beginning lectures— "Gentlemen . . . ." Men students reacted differently— "O maidens whose seat at the lecturer's feet/Is a vision of heaven afar,/Do you know how you act on our nerves and distract/All of us because you're what you are?

opposite, bottom:

Women's College Principal and students, 1892 Complementing the admission of women was the founding of a non-denominational women's college in 1892. Miss Louisa MacDonald (1858-1949) the first Principal is seated centre, standing behind is Eleanor Madeline Whitfeld, seated (left) Dorothy Emma Harris, (right) Lucy Isabelle Flavelle, and in front Constance Elizabeth Harker. The present College building opened in 1894.

below:

Women students outside their Common Room, c.1892 (L. to R.) Emma Proctor, Joanna Barton, Elizabeth Proctor, fourth is not known. Converted from an early chemical laboratory, this room stood on the south side of the Quadrangle. Its facilities were meagre—a gas ring, tin dishes for washing up—if you were quick enough to grab one. When Adela Pankhurst spoke here c.1912 men students pelted the roof with stones in protest.

Men's Common Rooms, 1890's Until 1913 these two wooden buildings contained most of the social life of non-college students and some Union activities for all students. In an atmosphere redolent with stale tobacco smoke they talked, ate their buns, made tea, stole each other's spoons and sugar, fed the common room cat, talked, and caricatured their professors on the walls. The smaller room survives as a tennis club house near the Main Gates.

University grounds, c.1895 From a point near St. Andrew's College, this view shows part of the Royal Prince Alfred Hospital (left), and the Medical School on the distant right; trees border the embankment of the west and south edges of the Quadrangle area.

opposite:

Academic picnic at Medlow Caves, Blackheath, 1895 (L. to R. back row) Miss Harriott, H.E.Barff, Msgr. J.J.O'Brien (Rector of St. John's College), Minnie Roseby, Dr Julia Carlyle Thomas, Miss Harriott; (front row) Professor J.T.Wilson (anatomy), Professor G.A.Wood (history), Constance Harker, Mrs Trechmann, Miss Britten, Dr A.P.Trechmann (lecturer in French and German).

below:

Biology (L) and Engineering (R) buildings, 1893 These buildings occupied roughly the site of the present Old Union and Refectory. In 1896 the benefaction of Sir Peter Nicol Russell, a Sydney industrialist, was recognised by the attachment of his name to the School of Engineering.

Engineering students, 1892 William Henry Warren (1852-1926), first Professor of Engineering, is seated centre. Though at this time part of the Faculty of Science, engineers clearly symbolised their separate identity through their banner design of the old Hawkesbury railway bridge (built 1889). (Names of the students cannot be identified, but a list of engineering students for 1892 is given in Appendix.)

Biological Laboratory, 1895 L. to R. Professor John Thomas Wilson (Anatomy), J.P.Hill (Demonstrator in Biology, and C.J.Martin (Demonstrator in Physiology).

right:

Anyone for tennis? c.1890 A mixed double is in progress on the further court, a singles game on the nearer. For more adventurous sportswomen at this time a women's Boat Club offered sailing on the harbour. Slow exposure of the camera film has caused some double image in this photograph.

below:

First year physiography excursion, c.1898 Edgeworth David (1858-1934), Professor of Geology, smiles gently amid a sea of straw deckers whose bands gaily sport the University arms; an upturned brim (3rd from R.) might suggest an early "ocker" outlook. (For names of people in this photograph, see Appendix.)

The Chancellor, Sir Normand MacLaurin, congratulates the first woman law graduate, Ada Emily Evans, 1902 Teaching for an undergraduate law course began in 1890 under Professor Pitt Cobbett, but before the intrepid Miss Evans could enrol, the lack of precedent for a woman student-at-law had to be overcome. Even when her degree was conferred, State laws still debarred her from practising as a barrister until 1921 when they were amended—partly through her own crusading.

Military Review on University Grounds, 24 May 1895 N.S.W. Troops celebrate Queen Victoria's birthday with a *Feu-de-joie*. The carriages of official guests are in the middle distance, beyond and to the right, laundry of the hospital dries fitfully in the rain.

Golden Jubilee Celebrations, 1902 To mark the 50th anniversary of its inauguration the University was host to representatives of overseas and Australian universities and Registrar Barff wrote a short history. Judge Alfred Backhouse, a former Vice-Chancellor, glances to the camera as Professor J.W.Gregory of Melbourne, and Professor Liversidge, enter the Quadrangle garden party.

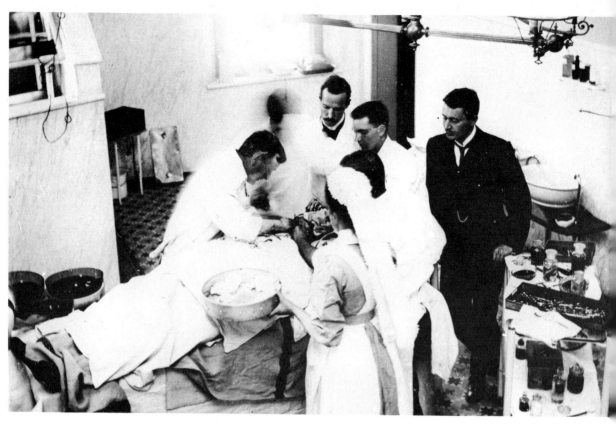

Surgical operation, possibly c.1905   This student
observation theatre in the Royal Prince Alfred Hospital
has now been demolished. The observer on the right
is possibly the youthful Charles Bickerton Blackburn.

Student bicyclists, c.1900   At the turn of the century,
bicycling was a sport and a cheap form of transport.
Straw deckers and bicycle clips round trouser bottoms
were "in" gear for the road.

The University from George Street south (now Broadway), near Railway Square, c.1900 No pollution count was needed for this level of traffic, but the washing of omnibus horses in Victoria Park just below the University was said to be an unforgettable experience for those who were passing by.

Inter-Varsity Cricket Team, 1903 This team played against Melbourne. J.W.Woodburn, the Captain, graduated Bachelor of Engineering in the same year. (L. to R. back row) G.C.James umpire, E.J.Gregson, A.D.Fisher, H.E.Manning, C.Bannerman umpire, M.M.MacEncroe scorer; (Middle row) Dr G.R.C.Clarke, D.C.Close, J.W.Woodburn, S.H.Harris, E.F.Waddy, L.Cowlinshaw; (Front row) A.Verge, S.W.Powell.

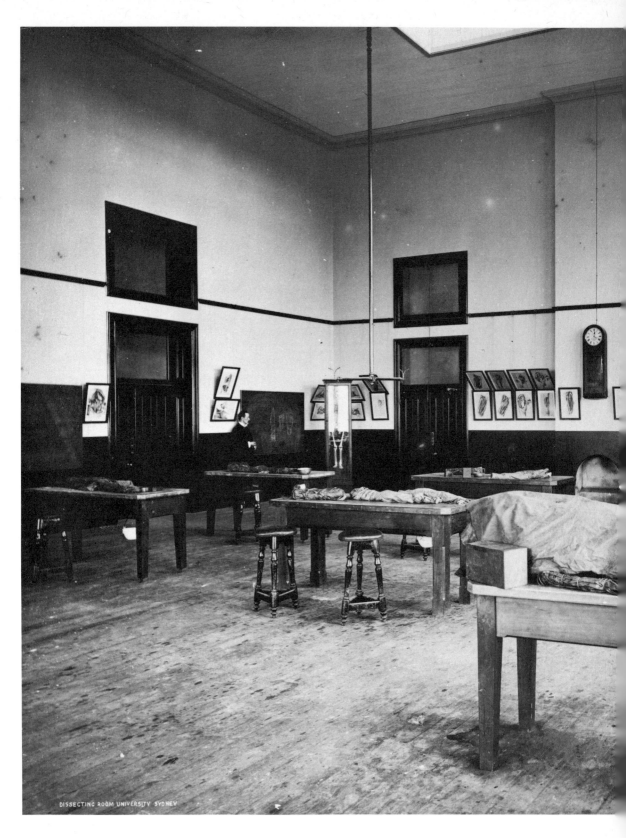

DISSECTING ROOM UNIVERSITY SYDNEY

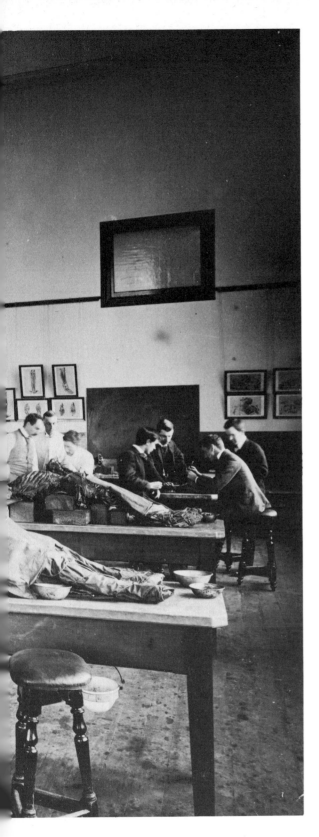

Dissecting Room of Medical School, c.1900
Amid these relatively primitive conditions of
hygiene, senior students (known as prosectors)
prepared dissections for teaching and research.

"Commem." Day floats, c.1910 These floats,
assembling outside the first Engineering building,
celebrate the success of Shackleton's Antarctic
Expedition in which Edgeworth David played a notable
part.

opposite:

"Commem." Day procession, c.1910 Beginning as a
modest display of faculty banners carried into the
Great Hall by students on Commemoration Day,
festivities grew to a long cavalcade of topical and
satirical floats that wound its rowdy way through
Sydney streets. In this photograph, trencher-capped Arts
students march beneath their banner—*Floreant
Artes*—through Railway Square; city urchins enjoy some
reflected glory of the (Bavarian?) band.

"Commem." Day caricatures, c.1912 (1) Bare feet,
beard and long hair "send up" William James Chidley
(1860-1916), the Sydney sex, health and dress eccentric,
who was just fifty years ahead of his time; (2) Empire
Day (founded 24 May 1905) is spoofed by a military
looking transvestite. So many Commem. Day stunts were
men impersonating women that in 1921 the Professorial
Board ruled against such behaviour. (*Note:* Women
did not take part in "Commem." Day until c.1930.)

Building the first Fisher Library, c.1907 Prompted by Thomas Fisher's bequest in 1885 for library purposes, the N.S.W. Government later made funds available for a library building. The highly decorated Gothic style sought to balance Blacket's Great Hall diagonally across the Quadrangle. This photograph, taken inside the future reading room area, shows stone carvers at work.

The completed Fisher Library, c.1910 Open in 1909, the new Library was named for Thomas Fisher, a Sydney businessman, who is said to have enjoyed sauntering through the University grounds. An adjoining bookstack and offices formed part of the project which also included an initial small section of cloisters. The building is now known as the MacLaurin Hall. The photograph also shows the women's Common Room.

Walter Liberty Vernon (1846-1914) As N.S.W. Government Architect, Vernon was responsible for the design and erection of the first Fisher Library and stacks; his designing hand is also seen in the Anderson Stuart Building extensions, the old Law School in Phillip St., and the Union (Holme Building).

"In" Gear for men, c.1910
Photographed on the front steps of
the Macleay Museum (obscured since
the 1920's by the Botany Building)
these young men conform to
popular fashion—straw deckers,
watch chains, high collars, walking-
canes, and for a few the latest thing
—trouser cuffs. An academic joke
of the time referred to students
turning up trouser bottoms because it
was raining in London.

The Senate Room, c.1912 The former library room with its internal oriel window looking into the Great Hall was converted to a formal meeting room for the Senate and other committees. However, the regular meetings of the Senate continued to be held at University Chambers (the Law School) in Phillip St., until November 1957. At this time the Senate comprised 24 Fellows; a Fellow representing the students was not included until 1937.

Quadrangle area, c.1912 Apparently taken about mid-day, this photograph gives some idea of daily life outside the lecture room—women students enjoy tennis, men eat their sandwiches outdoors and leave some litter in the process. The small domed building housed a telescope and was known as

"Noah's Ark
Where mixed classes after dark
Watch the planets, especially Venus."

Miss Katherine Winifred Dwyer (1863?-1949) Miss Dwyer was the first woman member of the Senate, appointed in 1916 by the Holman Government in response to the increasing number of women students. The first woman elected to the Senate was Dr Constance D'Arcy in 1919.

"Commem." Day Procession at the corner of Bridge and George Streets, 1920's The spirit of "Commem." Day was to "Fling to the winds the mortar-board . . . and turn all Sydney upside down". The City fathers, the police, and the University Senate resisted as best they could, mainly by denying permission to go through the city. Despite being targets for flour, water and other objects, the public remained curious and indulgent for the most part.

left:

Men's Union Common Room, c.1914 In 1911 the old debating Union was reformed to provide club facilities in a new building opened in 1913. The part of Ernest Rudolph Holme (1871-1954), Professor of English Literature, in this development was recorded in song at Union dinners—"Who built the blanky Union? Why, E.R.Holme." In 1975 the building was named in his honour.

Completion of south side of Quadrangle, c.1917 This extension provided a periodicals room for the Library (now the Professorial/Academic Board Room) and lecture rooms and offices below; it also continued the range of cloisters begun in 1908.

above:

Engineering workshop staff, 1916 The growth of teaching involving technical equipment, resources and complex premises, has been accompanied by a growth of professional technicians and attendant support staff. This photograph shows (L. to R. back row) Harold Baldwin, John Reid, George Fountain, Cecil McHatton; (front) Herbert Middlehurst, Boyd Connolley.

right:

Burying the hatchet, 1917 Weary of "sitting on the seats of the future" and envious of the new Union building for men, women formed their own Union in 1914 and agitated for new building for their use. It was achieved with the opening of Manning House in 1917 which also resolved the feeling between the two sexes. The central figure is E.R.Holme and on his right Miss Isabel Fidler ("Fido"), Tutor to women students and tutelary deity of Manning House.

Refectory in basement of first Fisher Library, c.1920
Opened in 1914, the Refectory was located in the area now the Anthropology Dept. It was strong on baked custard and date pudding. Dinners such as this one of the Evening Students Association (formed 1900) were formal affairs; Barff and Holme loom avuncularly in the background.

below:

Junction of Parramatta and City Roads, c.1926
"Getting to Uni." by electric tram was cheap at student concession rates—one penny (.8c) a section, six sections for three pence (2.5c).

Visit of the Prince of Wales, 13 June 1920   The spirit
of the Empire was greatly fired by the experience of the
Great War and the world tour of the Prince of Wales
(later King Edward VIII, Duke of Windsor) was
partly an extension of this feeling. At the University
the Prince was awarded an Honorary LL.D., but later
confessed to students that he was, in fact, like them—
still an undergraduate (of Oxford).

*The Vice-Chancellor, Registrar, Yeoman Bedell, and
attendant staff, c.1924*   The University Amendment Act
of 1924 provided for the appointment of a full-time
executive head of the University who would be styled
the Vice-Chancellor. The first holder of this office was
Professor Mungo MacCallum. He is seated in the centre,
and on his left is Mr W.A.Selle (1888-1968) who was
Registrar 1924-47, and Mr W.Barber (d.1948) who
was Yeoman Bedell 1914-40 is on his right. (For names
of attendants, see Appendix.)

The University Scouts' headquarters, 1920's Once the men's Common Room, this building was moved to a site behind the Zoology and Agriculture buildings for the Scouts. In 1900 the University Volunteer Rifle Corps was formed and in 1903 (prompted by Boer War strategy) it was renamed as Scouts. In 1927 it became the University Regiment. The Scouts' song went—

> We are soldiers grim and gory,
> (Zim-zerim-zim-zim-zim-zim)
> Fit to fight for death or glory,
> At our head 'mid trumpets' blare
> Rides that gallant officaire
> Major R.C.Simpson — wow!

page: 85

The University Company, 1918 About 1,700 members of the University had enlisted for service in the Great War by 1918, but the Undergraduates Association felt recruitment would be encouraged by the formation of a University Company. Examinations were held early for those who enlisted and the company (of 180) went into camp in the University grounds in September 1918. The signing of the Armistice cancelled the company's projected embarkation on 16 November. (A list of the company and of all servicemen was published in 1939 in the University *Book of Remembrance*.)

opposite, top:

Engineering laboratory, c.1925 Students and equipment in the new Engineering School which opened in 1909 (since 1971 renamed the Woolley Building). Contemporary students sung the praises of the Professors of mechanical, civil and electrical engineering in the lines

> And here's to rivets and boilers and cams
> And stresses and strains and shearing;
> And here's to Warren and Barraclough,
> And Madsen and others, but that's enough,
> To show that we need the best of stuff,
> To teach us our Engineering.

right:

"Lab. work", c.1926 Medical students, possibly at an examination, on the top floor of the Anderson Stuart Building north wing. A somewhat cynical attitude toward examinations was expressed in a contemporary student song which claimed

> "The Profs have issued a bold decree
> That fifty per cent must fail . . .
> It doesn't matter what you be,
> Med or Greaser or Law."

left:

Examinations in the Great Hall, c.1925   A tense and crucial time for students, the examination system has been a constant feature of University training. In this photograph natural lighting is supplemented by gas brackets on the walls; the present electric lamps were installed in 1928 and it was once an exercise for engineering students to calculate the level of illumination they gave at examination desk level.

right:

John Irvine Hunter (1898-1924)   Hunter's brief life, crowded with academic success and activity, is recalled still with warmth and sadness. Made Associate Professor of Anatomy upon graduation in 1920 he was appointed to the chair in 1923, the youngest professor ever. He died from enteric fever while overseas.

The fresher's ordeal, 1923   This cartoon from the Undergraduates' Association magazine *Hermes* seems like a piece of male conceit; more likely the roles were reversed judged from a student song about women's fashions—
  Where transparent stockings and clothes labelled shocking
  Make men feel life still can be borne.
Established in 1886, *Hermes* at first excluded women from its contributions and its management; by the 1930's its elegantly printed pages often carried poems by Muir Holburn and James Macauley; in recent years its publication has been erratic.

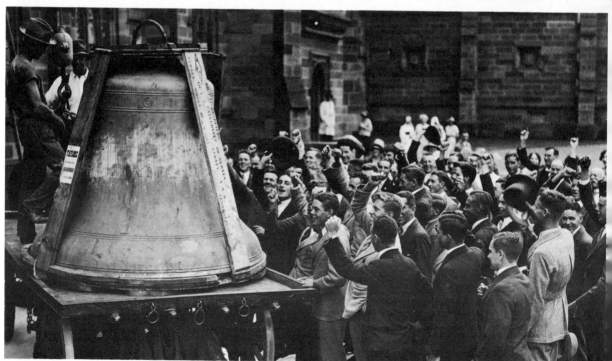

75th Anniversary Dinner, 1927 On 8 July 1927 the University opened an
appeal for £250,000 to provide additional income. One fund raising
project was an anniversary dinner on 11 October 1927 in the Great Hall;
The Governor-General, Lord Stonehaven, and the Prime Minister,
Mr S.M.Bruce, attended. The champagne and good food are said to have
mellowed "the terror of the classics students", Professor F.A.Todd, but
there was some difference of opinion among other guests about the
pronunciation of the Latin grace.

opposite, top:

University grounds, c.1930 This view is from the Royal Prince Alfred
Hospital across the site of the present Blackburn Building (opened 1933)
to the long range of St. Paul's College (right) and Wesley College
(centre) established 1910; the Physics Building in white stucco is at left.
Virtual completion of the Quadrangle buildings has apparently driven
lawn tennis players to this more remote location.

Arrival of the A.I.F. Bell, 1928 Members of the University who served
in the Great War were commemorated in a War Memorial Carillon
subscribed for by the University community and the public and erected in
the Great Tower. The 62 bells were cast in England by John Taylor & Co.,
and the carillon was inaugurated on Anzac Day 1928. The A.I.F. Bell,
weighing 4½ tons, is the largest in the carillon.

91

Conferring of degrees in the Great Hall, 28 April 1928 At this ceremony about 300 degrees and some diplomas were awarded in all faculties except medicine. Arts continued to account for most graduates. From the first conferring in 1856 to 1928 10,660 degrees had been conferred.

A Wilkinson flourish   Much of the architectural
decoration that Professor Leslie Wilkinson (1882-1973)
employed on university buildings had meaning beyond
mere ornamentation. This lantern set high above the
Administration Building and topped with a weather vane,
adds interest and inspiration to the skyline.

below:

Wilkinson's sketch for the Chemistry Block, 1923
There is a strong sense of Mediterranean tradition in
this rough design in which Wilkinson remodelled and
enlarged old buildings and incorporated the classical
facade of the old C.B.C. Bank building from
George St., Sydney. Wilkinson's influence as Australia's
first Professor of Architecture was considerable; student
songs cheekily commemorate his sobriquet Whitewashing
Leslie.

*Opening of School of Public Health and Tropical
Medicine, 4 March 1930*   A joint undertaking of the
Commonwealth Dept. of Health and the University of
Sydney, the School's building was designed by Leslie
Wilkinson (standing 3rd from L.). Sitting (from L.)
are Prof. J.C.Windeyer, Dean of Faculty of Medicine,
Dr R.S.Wallace, Vice-Chancellor, Sir William Cullen,
Chancellor, the Hon. F.Anstey, Minister for Health,
the Hon. K. Arthur, N.S.W. Minister for Health,
Dr J.H.L.Cumpston, Commonwealth Director-General
of Health, and Dr Harvey Sutton first Director
of the School.

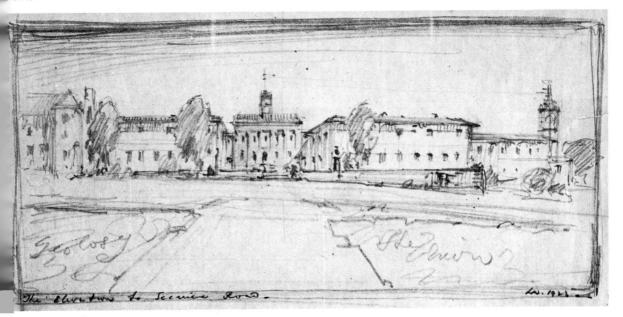

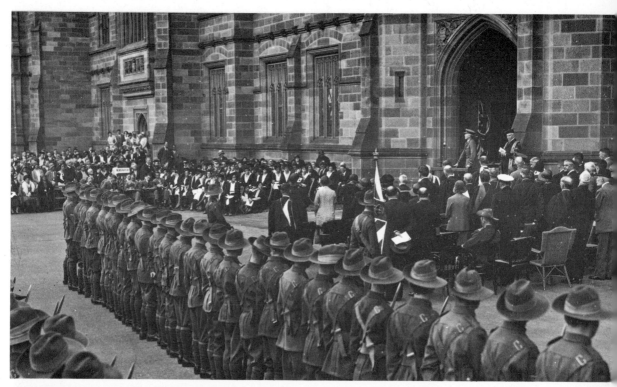

English lecture in Great Hall, 1932   The lecturer is Professor John Le Gay
Brereton (1871-1933) who had earlier been University Librarian.
A graduate of the University, Brereton was a noted Elizabethan scholar,
poet, and a staunch friend of Henry Lawson. Out of acoustical courtesy
perhaps, women still occupy the front seats, though Brereton is using an
early public address system (speaker top left). The organ (installed 1882)
has been removed for rebuilding.

opposite, top:

Unveiling of the Great War Honour Rolls, 11 November 1931   The
University Regiment forms a Guard of Honour for the Governor of N.S.W.,
Sir Philip Game. In his address, the Governor said that Australians had
fought 12,000 miles away "in the pursuit of the ideals of eternal truth".

Dedication of the Honour Rolls, 11 November 1931   The Anglican
Archbishop of Sydney, the Rt. Rev. John C. Wright, conducts the service
while the Governor and the Chancellor, Sir William Cullen, look on.
Writing of University men who served as officers in the Great War,
C.E.W. Bean said "hard-grained bush and wharf workers were ready to
follow them anywhere".

above:

University Regiment at Holdsworthy, 1939   A few
months before the outbreak of the 1939-1945 War the
Regiment is inspected by its Honorary Colonel,
Lord Wakehurst, Governor of N.S.W., accompanied by
the Commanding Officer, Lt.-Col. (later Major-General
Sir Victor) Windeyer. A graduate of the University,
Sir Victor Windeyer served with distinction during the
war; he held the office of Deputy-Chancellor during 1954-58.

Lecturers' Association, 1935   Members of the
Association process through the Quadrangle to lay a
wreath at the Honour Rolls, Armistice Day 1935, led by
the President, E.F.Campbell. Formed late in 1929 the
Association had as its objects "the advancement of
education and research . . . safeguarding the interests of
its members . . . seeking the utmost goodwill and
co-operation of all members of the University of
Sydney". The Association is now called the Sydney
Association of University Teachers.

Opening of The McGarvie Smith Animal Husbandry Farms, Badgerys Creek, 8 September 1938 One of the University's many external properties, the farm was paid for with funds from the McGarvie Smith Institute. It was acquired for the use of the Faculty of Veterinary Science whose foundation professor, J.D.Stewart, spoke at the opening ceremony.

below:
Student Voluntary Training Corps, 1940 The corps was organised by lecturers and students in the Faculty of Arts who received elementary training in rifle and squad drill from members of the Regiment on Oval No. 2. An A.R.P. unit was also established for the surveillance of University grounds.

First degrees at New England University College, 1941 The College was established in 1937 in association with the University of Sydney and opened in 1938. In this photograph the Chancellor, Sir Percival Halse Rogers, admits the first graduate, Miss Elizabeth Craigie, to the degree of Bachelor of Arts. The College became an autonomous University in 1954.

Students' Representative Council, 1944-1945 Men's and women's undergraduates associations had been formed in the 19th century, but in 1929 the S.R.C., based on faculty representation, was formed to give a more effective voice to student needs and views. In 1943 Miss Maude McDade (front row, 2nd from R.) became the first woman president of the Council. (See Appendix for list of names).

right:

The Stars and Stripes waving over Oval No. 1, 1944 United States military police forces were camped in the University grounds during the 1939-1945 War. This photograph was taken at a Citation Day Mass Presentation, Brigadier-General Rilea taking the salute.

below:

Special war work at the University, 1945 W.A.A.F.'s working in the former Electrical Engineering Dept. (now Badham Building) on war work; University staff and resources were employed in a number of war projects.

Revue ballet, 1941 From the 1930's the staging of a university revue became a notable part of "Commem." celebrations. Organised by the Students' Representative Council, some revue segments were prepared and presented by the colleges. This ballet rehearses in the old Union Hall which opened in 1916 and was demolished in 1961; the site is now occupied by the Union Theatre.

PART IV

Exploding
1946 - 1975

In the years after 1945 the influx of ex-servicemen and women studying under the Commonwealth Reconstruction Training Scheme (over 4,000 in 1948) swelled the student population to nearly 10,800. The Australian Government helped the University meet this pressure by providing funds for new buildings and equipment as well as subsidies for recurrent costs. Collaboration between the Australian Government and the University was not new; it had begun as early as 1911 with the School of Public Health and Tropical Medicine, and from 1936 university research had been assisted by Commonwealth funds. The money provided in connection with the Training Scheme greatly assisted the running of the University generally but about 1951 the slowing down of this operation seemed to imply an inevitable withdrawal of support just at a time when costs were rising. Recognising this situation the Australian Government from 1951 to 1957 continued its financial support of the University through a system of grants based on the University's income, and from 1958 (following the

Murray Report) on a more regular basis through the Australian Universities Commission which allocated funds on a basis of triennial development proposals and as part of an overall development plan for all Australian universities. In 1951 the Australian Government instituted a generous system of scholarships, and since 1974 has subsidised the University for the cost of all student fees and so made university education free to the student.

In the early and mid-1950's there was a drop in the number of students (less than 7,000 in 1953), due in part to the lower birth-rate of the Depression years, though perhaps the New South Wales University of Technology (from 1958 the University of New South Wales) now drew off some potential students. But this falling off in numbers was only a temporary situation; by 1961 the number of students had increased to over 12,500. The triennial support of the Australian Government from 1958 made it possible for the University to meet this remarkable growth, especially in expansion beyond its original boundaries into the adjoining suburb of Darlington.

By 1968 the number of students had reached more than 16,500 and it was predicted in the same year that the number would grow even larger because the rapid growth in knowledge had created the need for more students to continue in post-graduate work. The situation was referred to as a "research explosion". By 1975 the student population stood at 17,700 of whom 2,750 were post-graduates, supported by about 3,500 academic, administrative and other staff. The University was assuming some of the characteristics of a small city; it possessed its own newspaper (established in 1969), car parking and pollution problems.

There were also some other problems peculiar to the super-university. Academics and students alike found it demanding to keep up with developments in a multi-professorial school or department, difficult to appreciate all that was going on in the faculty, and very nearly impossible to comprehend any longer what the whole exercise was really all about—*universitas*. Some academic staff were said to find it easier to communicate with colleagues overseas than with academics in another discipline who were only one floor away. Meetings of faculties, boards and committees proliferated and took up more and more time and produced more and more minutes and reports for which there seemed less and less time to read. To improve communication and help administration, more undergraduate students were brought on to the Senate, Academic Board, and Faculty bodies, though they still claimed to be excluded from the real power of decision-making and sometimes expressed their feelings on particular issues through noisy protest demonstrations. And over all this loomed the increasing and necessary presence of the Australian Government through its financial patrimony.

But the super-university also brought economies of scale and a rich variety of experience. Students could choose from a broad range of courses that included Hindu social institutions, environmental issues and politics, advanced gas dynamics, econometric method, hospital pharmacy, law and social justice, and the age of medieval chivalry. The range of student social life embraced such diverse interests as the Speleological Society, Science Fiction Association and Women's Liberation. Far from disappearing under the pressure of all this activity, some traditional ceremonies actually increased. Fourteen Conferring of Degrees ceremonies were held in 1975 providing a bright spectrum of academic dress—twenty-one hood edgings for Bachelors, from white fur to amber and crimson or purple and gold silk, eighteen colours for Masters including brick red for architecture, and twelve kinds of festal gowns with black velvet bonnets and gold cord for doctors.

In 1856 the first graduates of the University had to subscribe to two promises before their degrees were conferred — that they would respect all the laws, regulations, privileges and liberties of the University, and that they would always promote the peace and harmony of the University. Though no longer required by regulation to make these promises, most graduates in 1975 would probably agree that some of those conditions are at least conducive, if not vital, to the future development and continued independence of the University.

left:

Settlement fete, 1947 Founded in 1891, the University Settlement sought to involve university people in social issues. Early work was done at Millers Point and Woolloomooloo and in 1925 the Chippendale properties were acquired. Funds for the work were raised by fetes like this one held by the Settlement Mothers' Club. Mr Frank Albert, music publisher and University benefactor, stands on the right. (See Appendix for list of others in the photograph.)

Asian students, 1954 Many overseas students have studied at the University since 1945, some under the Colombo Plan which began in 1950, others by private means. This photograph includes students from Thailand, China, Ceylon, East Pakistan, Nepal, and Malaya.

below:

"Honi Soit" staff, 1949 Established in 1929 as a weekly journal of student opinion, *Honi Soit* has appeared regularly since then. Somewhat given to *ex parte* views and more recently to dramatic *exposé*, the paper has provided early training for some noted journalists and writers. This office was located behind the Macleay Museum. People in the news are (L. to R. first two unknown) Shirley Harris, Jenny Nisbet, Jenny Snelling, Dick Woodward, Peter Lazar, Michael Baume, Michael Lazar, Peter Tranter, David Ross, and H.Brunen.

Centenary Celebrations in the Great Hall, 1952
Centenary celebrations were held in 1950 to mark the
incorporation of the University, in 1951 to mark the
first Senate meeting, and in 1952 major celebrations
marked the inauguration of the University. The Chief
Justice of N.S.W., Sir Kenneth Street, a graduate of the
University, is shown here delivering the Centenary
oration, the Chancellor, Sir Charles Blackburn presiding.

right:

Visit of H.R.H. The Duke of Edinburgh, 1954 At a
reception in the Great Hall, Prince Philip is shown
talking with the Rt. Hon. H.V.Evatt, former Minister for
External Affairs and High Court Judge, Fellow of the
Senate, and a notable graduate in law and arts. Other
Fellows of the Senate (L. to R.) are Sir Charles
McDonald, Miss Fanny Cohen, Professor F.A.Bland,
Dr H.Wyndham, Mr A.Landa.

Science School for high school students, 1962
Exploration of outer space in the 1950's added a new urgency to science education in which the University's Science Foundation for Physics directed by Professor H.Messel has played a notable part. In this photograph the American rocket expert, Dr Wernher von Braun addresses students. (See Appendix for list of other people in photograph.)

opposite: bottom:
Expansion of the University, 1966 Post-war
accommodation needs brought about the acquisition of
property in adjoining Darlington from 1958; in 1959
the first building (for Architecture) was erected. This
photograph shows (middle distance) Engineering
buildings erected 1961-63. In the foreground is the
Darlington Primary School established in 1877.

right:
Surryville Ballroom, 1920's Its fast sprung
floor once enjoyed wide acclaim among
dancers whose permanent waves and push-back
hair styles remain faultless on this warm night.
The shirt-sleeved figure (L.) is thought to be
the lessee, Mr Owens.

International House site inspection, 1965
The Australian Universities Commission and
University administrators inspect the site and
model for the new residential house for
overseas students. (L. to R.) Professor J.Still,
Sir Stephen Roberts (Vice-Chancellor),
Professor W.M.O'Neil (Deputy Vice-
Chancellor), Professor N.S.Bayliss,
Mr M.W.Jackson, Mr K.R.McInnes, Professor
A.D.Trendall (back to camera), Sir Leslie
Martin (Chairman of A.U.C.—obscured),
Mr A.R.Winston, Mr D.Dexter,
Mr R.A.Simpson. International House opened
in 1967. The project, initially sponsored by Rotary
was assisted by Asian Governments.

Old houses, Darlington, c.1965   The two-storied house (now demolished) stood on the corner of Alma and Codrington Streets, and was associated with Thomas Fisher, benefactor of the University Library. The lace verandah posts were cast in the Sydney foundry of P.N.Russell, another benefactor.

opposite:

Lallah-Rookh Hotel, 1960's   Now demolished, from 1885 or earlier it stood on the corner of City Road and Codrington Streets. A popular pub with staff and students it was frequently celebrated in song—
>Here in the darkling depths of night,
>Down at the Lallah Rookh,
>In Bacchic revels the Profs. delight,
>Down at the Lallah Rookh.

The new Fisher Library commenced, 1961   The Prime Minister, the Rt. Hon. R.G.Menzies, unveils the foundation plaque of a new undergraduate and research library of 9 floors. It was through the initiative of the Menzies Government that Commonwealth funds became readily available to all universities. In the background is the Chancellor, Sir Charles Blackburn, and on the right the Registrar, Miss Margaret Telfer.

College life, 1960's   Traditional college life is maintained in St. Paul's dining hall with high table and academic dress. In 1928 the College magazine observed "Young men in College usually have their first drink in their Second Year. It is an experiment every man must make in the course of his education. If the effects are too much for him, so much the better that he is within the precincts of the College and among friends."

Wesley College Chapel, 1966 The traditional place of religious worship in college life was restated in 1965 by an enlargement of the chapel which was originally opened in 1917. In 1969 Wesley College broke with tradition by adopting a co-educational policy.

left:

University Chambers, 167 Phillip St., Sydney, 1966 Law lectures had long been associated with the legal *purlieus* of Phillip St. and the courts. In 1913 the University acquired Wigram Chambers and enlarged it above the cornice line as a permanent law school; in 1937-38 extensions to the law school were built in Elizabeth St. In 1969 a single new law school building was opened on the corner of King, Phillip and Elizabeth Streets.

Law School Library, 1966 The Elizabeth St. extensions provided space for this library accommodation which was under the direction of Miss M.Dalrymple Hay as Assistant Librarian and Clerk to the Faculty.

Opening of Merewether Building, 14 June 1966 The increasing involvement of the Australian Government in the development of the University is evidenced here by the presence of Senator John Gorton (centre), Minister for Works and Housing. Also shown are (L. to R.) Sir Stephen Roberts (Vice-Chancellor), Mr W.H.Maze (Deputy-Principal), the Chancellor (Sir Charles McDonald), Professor S.J.Butlin, and the Rev. B.Wyllie (Deputy-Chancellor).

Chemistry lecture, 1960's The pressure of increased enrolments is seen at this lecture in the new Chemistry Building (opened 1960) where even the aisle steps are fully occupied.

Physics I laboratory, probably early 1960's   This laboratory has now been converted to other teaching purposes.

left:

Miss Margaret Telfer (d.1974), Registrar   A graduate of the University and a former Adviser to Women Students, Miss Telfer was Registrar from 1955 to 1967, the first woman in Australia to hold such a post. In 1969 the University conferred on Miss Telfer the honorary degree of Doctor of Letters.

opposite:

The Professorial Board in session, 1960's   From 1883 to 1975 the Professorial Board was the chief academic body of the University; in July 1975 it was replaced by a more widely representative body, including students. In this photograph the Chairman, Professor W.M.O'Neil is flanked (L.) by the Vice-Chancellor (Sir Stephen Roberts), and (R.) by the Registrar (Miss M.Telfer). The board room was formerly the periodicals room of the first Fisher Library.

The last Matriculation Ceremony, 1969   The vastly swollen annual intake of students (about 4,000 at this time) eroded the closely-knit feeling of community that gave meaning to such ceremonies as Matriculation in former years. In this photograph the Registrar (Mr H.McCredie) and the Associate Registrar (Mr R.B.Fisher) mount the dais steps in the Great Hall, preceded by the Yeoman Bedell (Mr J.Brook).

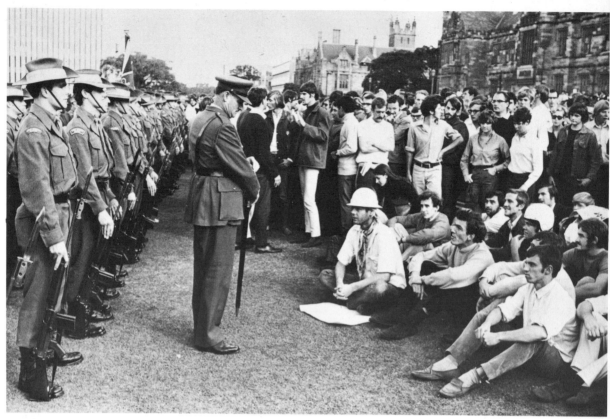

Confrontation on the Front Lawn, 1 May 1969 The University Regiment Guard of Honour present at a Conferring of Degrees ceremony is confronted by activist students. A tense situation developed involving groups of students. The late 1960's and early 1970's were characterised by student activism over political, social and university issues.

below:

Inter-Faculty Rugby League, 1971 Though faculty banners and flour fights are no longer seen, inter-faculty sport still preserves some of the former narrower loyalties of students as in this final match between Engineering and Economics on Oval No. 1.

opposite page:

Crowding in, 1970 First year students are welcomed by Mr Percy Allen, President of the S.R.C., at a Front Lawn ceremony.

all this spread:

Orientation Week market place, 1970's   A carnival tradition holds sway over the preliminary week of the first term of the academic year. Amid a heavy programme of lectures, music, entertainments, exhibitions and parties, dozens of student societies tout for membership in a temporary canvas market place on the front lawn and elsewhere.

Captain Harry Markham (c.1877-1924)   The work of the University has been greatly assisted by many generous benefactors. Names like McCaughey and Bosch occupy a central and honoured place in University history and nomenclature. Lesser known benefactors include Mrs Nellie Markham (1878-1969) who bequeathed her estate to the University in memory of her husband, Captain Harry Markham, an Australian-born master mariner who for 20 years piloted ships in Chinese waters.

opposite:

Vietnam Moratorium Meeting, 30 June 1971   Probably the largest crowd ever assembled on the Front Lawn, it included staff and students from other universities as well. The crowd later marched along Parramatta Road and Broadway to join other demonstrators in the city. The occasion marked the apogee of large-scale academic involvement in political affairs.

below:

"Commem." Day crowd in Australia Square, 1971 By the 1970's much of the original excitement and wit of "Commem." Day had vanished, student energy, perhaps, being drained off to more serious activist "demos". Fund-raising for charity gave the day some continued excuse, but the procession had become sadly truncated and tawdry and it was abandoned in 1975. This photograph was taken by Ross Pedrana, a student in Veterinary Science.

Photograph by
A.I.Kirillov.

all this page:.

How they looked in the 1970's "In" gear for students bore no necessary relation to economic conditions—(accelerated) faded denim and bare feet were favoured by affluent and indigent alike, and long hair did not always imply intellectual proclivities.

Wentworth Union dining room, 1974 The temporary Union facilities were replaced in 1972 by the first block of the Wentworth Union, named for W.C.Wentworth. All Union services are now administered by The University of Sydney Union, an amalgamation of the former men's and women's unions, which became effective on 1 January 1972 despite a small rear-guard action of some conservative male traditionalists.

"Getting to Uni.", 1974 For staff cars there was zoned and authorised parking—at a price; most students suffered the public transport and smog of Parramatta Road, but a few came by motor-bike, their heads encased in space-age helmets; determined environmentalists defied the heavy traffic on bicycles.

Where they lived, 1974 These buildings in Parramatta Road near the Main Gates offered shelter to some students. University Hall, formerly the University Hotel, has a medieval connotation and a certain peeling grandeur, but was not part of the University.

left:

Part of Sancta Sophia College, 1974 The most recent of the colleges (established 1929), Sancta Sophia is a Catholic College for women. This new wing was built in 1968.

opposite:

Escaping by television, 1974 The Union building in Science Road (named Holme Building in 1975) provides a television lounge for student viewing.

Communicating with closed circuit television, 1974 As the University grows bigger, electronic technology attempts to shrink it back to more manageable, if less personal, lecture size. The University Television Unit, established in 1964, also covers general events such as this address by the Chancellor during Orientation Week.

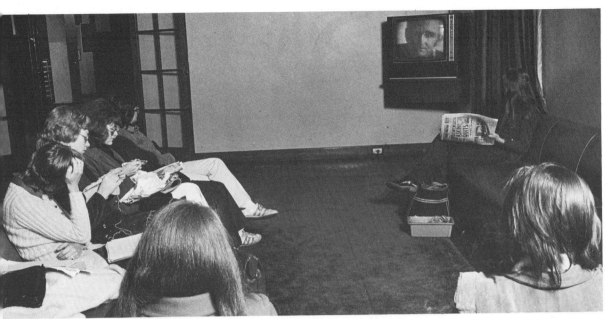

RESTORE UNION SERVICES AT OLD UNION
Free ISRAEL = RHODESIA = SETTLER STATES

opposite :

"Pooh" in Academe, 1974   A.A.Milne's children's stories attracted large audiences to the Wallace Lecture Theatre when lovingly interpreted by academics (L. to R.) John Roche, John Maze, Professor Frederick May, and Terry McMullen. The readings showed signs of becoming an annual student treat.

Polluting the passage, 1973   The walls of the new Wentworth Union are defaced by student grafitti; applied clandestinely in seconds with aerosol spray paint, its removal may take days.

right:

The newest architecture, 1974   The Bio-Chemistry building in the Darlington extension was designed by Stafford, Moor and Farrington, Sydney architects. Pre-cast panels of Nepean River gravel and off-forme concrete have been used in its external fabric.

The medium is the passage, 1974   The walls and steps of the subway below the Badham Building, Science Road, are available for moving fingers of all kinds. But you have to be quick to get the message—long before opening date *Much ado* will be obscured by Barbevino (BYOG) and Galapagos Duck.

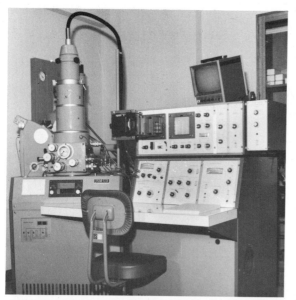

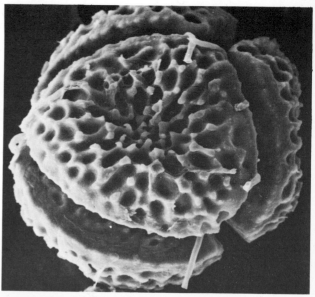

opposite:

Scanning electron microscope, 1975 This equipment assists scientific research in many areas. It operates by focusing a beam of electrons into a small spot on the specimen. By scanning the spot of electrons across the specimen and recording (for example) the number of back-scattered electrons as a function of time, differences in specimen composition or surface topography result in differences in the recorded signal. This signal can then be converted into an image of the specimen.

Liverwort spore (Riccia deserticola) image taken with the scanning electron microscope The spore is approximately 0.1 mm in diameter.

The Chancellor, Sir Hermann Black, and Sir Eric Ashby, 28 April 1973 At one time Professor of Botany in the University, later Vice-Chancellor of Cambridge University, Sir Eric (later Lord) Ashby is shown here being awarded the honorary degree of Doctor of Letters. The citation referred to Sir Eric as "a practical man with the power to see beyond the detailed problems of administration in a very complex organisation".

below:

Learning by closed circuit television, 1974 The profession of dentistry in N.S.W. was regularised by the Dental Act of 1900. Almost at once the University established a School of Dentistry and a dental hospital. In 1906 the first Bachelor of Dental Surgery degrees were conferred. The present dental laboratories in Chalmers St., Sydney, incorporate this television studio.

University bindery, 1974 Through its Services Department, the University provides a wide range of administrative services—printing, duplicating, binding, photography, stores and garage. Former factory buildings in the Darlington extension were adapted to house the Services Dept. in 1960.

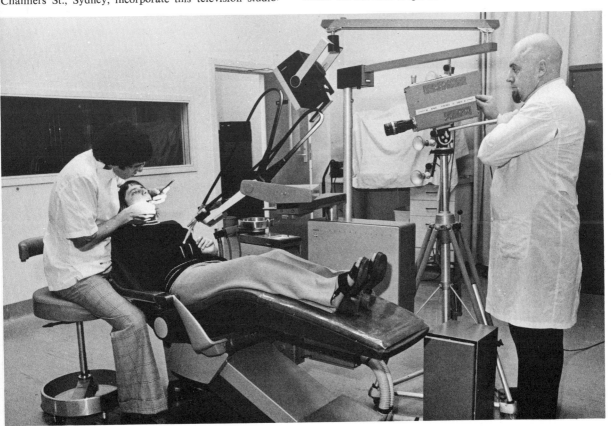

left:

University Computing Centre, 1974 Through the generosity of Sir Adolph Basser, SILLIAC, the first computer, was installed in the Physics School in 1956. In 1974 all computing operations were grouped in a new building in the Darlington extension. An essential part of scientific research, teaching, and administration in a large and complex university, the computer centre is also used by students as part of their course work.

Computed food, 1974 A series of vending machines in the Union Fishery present a rapid-service but non-arguable selection of food-alternatives to students in a hurry to catch up with learning.

opposite bottom:

Visit of the Australian Universities Commission, 1974 Increasing Australian Government financial support for the university has led to periodic inspections by members of the Commission when proposed triennial developments are discussed. In the front foreground (L.) the Vice-Chancellor, Professor B.R.Williams, stands with the Commission Chairman, Emeritus Professor P.H.Karmel (R.). Behind them (L. to R.) are Professor A.R. Main, Professor Leonie Kramer, Emeritus Professor F.B.Bull, and Mr C.Alcorso.

below:

The University Art Workshop, 1974 Sponsored jointly by the Faculty of Architecture and the Department of Fine Arts, the Art Workshop is an innovation in University teaching. In addition to providing formal instruction for students, its classes and facilities are made freely available for public use.

The Great Hall, 1974 Funds from the Eleanor Sophia Wood bequest provided this new organ in 1972, built by Rudolf von Beckerath of Hamburg and Mr R.Sharp of Sydney. Marble statues of J.H.Challis and W.C.Wentworth stand at left and right.

The Sports Centre Gymnasium, 1974 Completed in 1972, the Centre provides headquarters for the Women's Sports Association; its facilities are open to men and women students. This photograph shows women receiving instruction in gymnastics.

What it's all about? The
University's embossing seal is
applied to testamurs to be given
to graduates when their degrees
are conferred.

right:
Where it's at, 1975 An aerial
view showing the University
grounds linked by foot-bridges
(L.) across City Road and
(R.) Parramatta Road, to the
extension areas. Photograph by
Milton Kent & Son.

page 132

Vale, alma mater Sunlight on
the green lawns of the
Quadrangle, the warm brown
stones of the oldest buildings,
hold in the memory of all who
know them.

Appendix

Page 42 *University football team, 1871.* (L. to R. standing) W.Mathieson, A.P.Backhouse, M.McMahon, D.Fisher, J.Chisholm, V.B.Riley (Captain), J.Morrice, A.Yeomans, T.Powell, H.A.Richardson, D.Creed; (sitting) E.A.Sharpe, G.H.Fitzhardinge, J.J.Teece, G.Deas-Thomson, D.O'Connell, R.Teece, C.D.Dunne, F.D.Kent, J.Robertson.

Page 62 *Engineering students, 1892.* (1st year) R.F.Arnott, J.T.Dixon, W.J.Doak, E.W.Hedgeland, A.D.Hutchinson, C.F.Jackson, J.Nangle, E.S.Simpson, B.Sawyer, J.P.Wood; (2nd year) C.W.B.Jenkins, E.W.Nardin, H.P.Seale, A.R.Weigall, N.F.White; (3rd year) P.E.L.Hayley, W.H.Ledger, A.C.Millard, E.E.O'Brien, H.G.Trenchard.

Page 63 *First year physiography excursion, c. 1898.* (The following names supplied with the photograph, presumably L. to R.) 1 Miss Foy, 2 Paxton, 3 Palmer, 4 Lowmaker, 5 Holt, 6 Studdy, 7 Armstrong, 8 G.Bruce, 9 Parrett, 10 Stephenson, 11 W.Poole, 12 H.W.Myers, 13 [unident.], 14 E.H.Reynolds, 15 G.H.Wilson, 16 T.M. Taylor, 17 A.H.Mosley, 18 J.M.Newman, 19 Prof.E. David, 20 W.G.Woolnough, 21 H.Gould, 22 D.D.Dey, 23 C.F.Fiaschi, 24 A.Crowley, 25 R.E.Woolnough, 26 A.J.Petersen, 27 R.B.Reynolds, 28 R.C.Wilson, 29 J.W.Ryan, 30 J.Horsburgh, 31 P.H.Power, 32 P.L. West, 33 G.A.Buchanan, 34 D.J.Healey, 35 A.McInnes, 36 E.F.O'Sullivan, 37 R.S.Godsall, 38 H.S.Mort, 39 G. Skulthorpe, 40 W.J.Gorringe.

Page 83 *The Vice-Chancellor . . . and attendant staff, c.1924.* (L. to R. back row) 1 P.Sharp, 2 F.Wilson. 3 W.Whitham, 4 J.Stone, 5 [unident.], 6 W.Trenchard, 7 E.Hufton, 8 [unident.], 9 F.White, 10 [unident.], 11 A.Hewish.

Page 101 *S.R.C. 1944-1945.* (L. to R. back row) Miss A.Collins, Miss J.Mumford, G.C.Burfitt-Williams, A.C. Juleff, L.Cashen, E.J.Barton, Miss M.Jackson; (middle row) Miss D.Asher, J.Kitching, J.E.Nash, H.Nicolson, F.W.Fowler, Miss A.Raymond, Miss J.Wilson; (front row) H.Harrison, M.R.J.Salton (Secretary), Miss J.Chadwick (Vice-President), Miss M.Watt (President), P.Goodman (Vice-President), Miss M.McDade (Past President), L.Hume (Treasurer). Eight other members of the Council were absent when this photograph was taken.

Page 104 *Settlement fete, 1947.* (L. to R.) Mesdames Knight, Bowden, Andrews, Browning, Thwaites, Tasker, Gritten, Ross, Bathen, Gossilin, Thorpe, Tasker Jnr.

Page 106 *Science School for high school students, 1962.* (L. to R. front row) H.A.Showers (Secretary to the Foundation), O.A.Guth, Prof.H.Messel, R.Anderson (Projectionist), Prof.S.T.Butler, Prof.C.N.Watson Munro, Prof.C.B.A.McCusker, Dr. M.J.Buckingham.

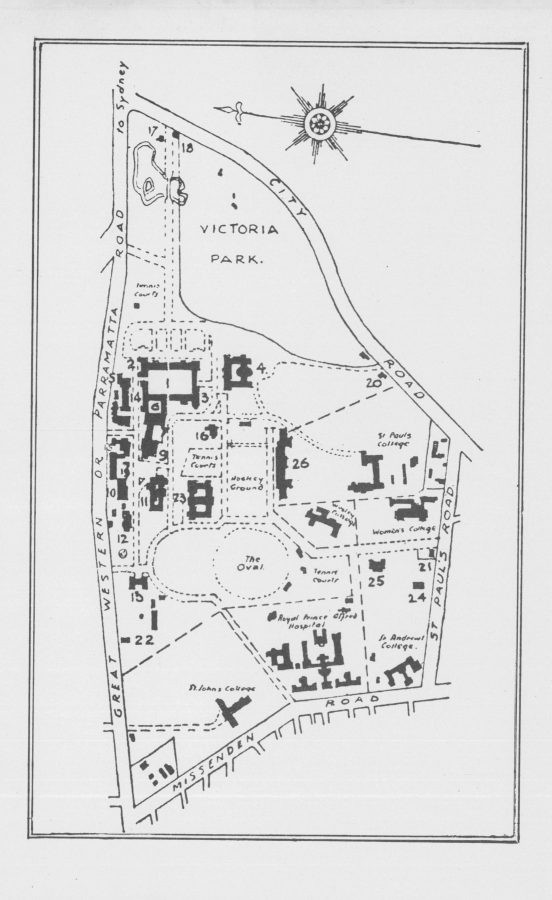